Plans and Patterns for Preschool

by
Karen Franz

illustrated by
Liza Sernett

cover illustration by
Steve Volavka

Publishers
T.S. Denison & Company, Inc.
Minneapolis, Minnesota 55431

T.S. DENISON & CO., INC.

No part of this publication may be reproduced or transmitted by any means, mechanical or electronic, including photocopy, recording, or stored in any information storage or retrieval system without permission from the publisher. Reproducible pages may be duplicated by the classroom teacher for use in the classroom, but not for commercial sale. Reproduction for an entire school or school system is strictly prohibited.

Standard Book Number: 513-02057-8
Plans and Patterns for Preschool
Copyright © 1991 by the T.S. Denison and Company, Inc.
Minneapolis, Minnesota 55431

INTRODUCTION

Plans and Patterns for Preschool provides Early Childhood teachers with ideas, patterns, plans, and activities for creating a stimulating classroom, both academically and visually. This book not only provides seasonal and thematic activities, but also provides ideas for decorating the classroom.

Plans and Patterns for Preschool will be a time-saver as well as a springboard for creativity. The suggestions in this book allow the teacher to make the most of the classroom and therefore give the best to the students.

Included in each monthly unit:
- Parent Bulletin Board
- Birthday Bulletin Board
- Calendar Ideas and Patterns
- Window Scenes
- Alphabet Learning Center
- Math Learning Center
- Science Learning Center
- Dramatic Play Learning Center
- Thematic/Classroom Activities
- Cubby Label Patterns
- Table Label Patterns
- Art Ideas and Patterns
- Literature Suggestions
- Music Suggestions

CONTENTS

SEPTEMBER

September   CALENDAR

WELCOME
BACK!

Sunday	Monday	Tuesday	Wednesday	Thursday	Friday	Saturday
		1	2	3	4	5
6	7	8	9			

Cut out the large "WELCOME BACK!" letters for September. Make sure that your students know what the words say.

Reproduce this schoolhouse pattern 30 times, coloring each one red and numbering them 1 to 30.

SEPTEMBER
BULLETIN BOARDS

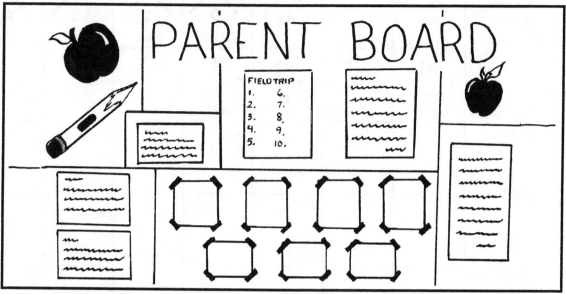

PARENT BOARD

Divide this month's Parent Board into sections to help familiarize the parents with the various kinds of information the Parent Board holds. Include pictures of your class and a few apples or pencils to decorate.

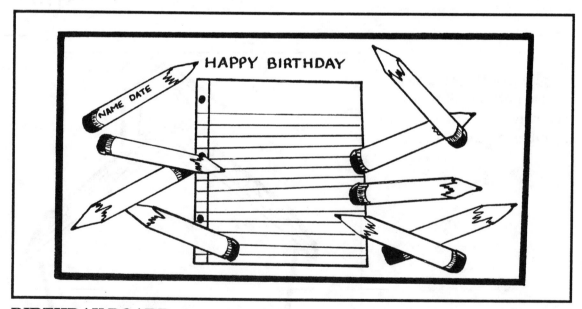

BIRTHDAY BOARD

Draw lines on a large sheet of white poster board or heavy paper to make a very large sheet of notebook paper. Cut large pencils out of yellow paper, coloring the erasers pink or green. Finally, label each pencil with a child's name and birthdate.

WINDOW SCENE

Cut large pieces of poster board or cellophane just a bit smaller than each window section. Cut a common shape out of each piece and tape to the window, allowing the sunshine to come through the shapes. This looks best when done with various colors of bright cellophane or paper.

CUBBY LABEL
Blackboard

10

TABLE LABEL
Crayon

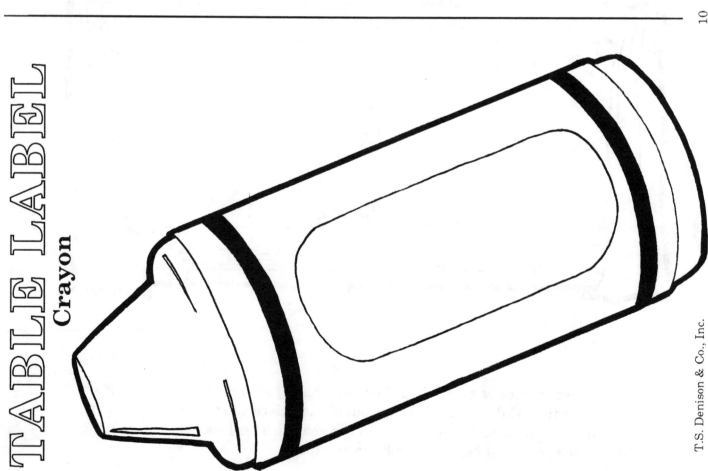

T.S. Denison & Co., Inc.

DRAMATIC PLAY

Create a Dramatic Play area in which your students can have a turn at being "the teacher." Include a teacher's desk, chalkboard, chalk, eraser, student's desks and plenty of crayons, paper and pencils.

SCIENCE

1 TASTE

BITTER:
Semi-sweet
Chocolate

SALTY:
Potato Chips

SOUR:
Lemons

SWEET:
Lollipops

Have a Tasting Party!

2 TOUCH

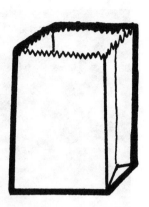

Put a number of familiar objects into a paper bag. While blindfolded, the children touch the objects and try to determine what the object is by the way it feels.

3 SMELL

Poke holes in the lids of non-transparent jars. Fill the jars with items that have odors familiar to the children. Examples would include peanut butter, lemons, chocolate. The children try to determine what is in the jar by its smell.

4 SIGHT

Blindfold one student at a time and ask him or her to do a simple *(yet safe!)* classroom activity, such as putting a toy away.

5 HEARING

Tape familiar sounds such as the telephone ringing, car honking, water running, etc. on a tape recorder and let the students identify the sounds.

MATH

1 2 3 4 5
6 7 8 9
10

COUNT EVERYTHING!

Count the number of children in each classroom, the number of tables in the room, the number of days in the week, etc.

Also have the children count during transition times and see how high everyone can count.

TRACING NUMBERS

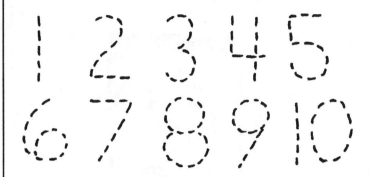

Draw outlines of the numbers from 1 to 10 and reproduce a number of copies for the children to practice tracing.

NUMBER STICKS

Enlarge each number between 1 and 10 for each child to color and then put on the appropriate number of stickers.

NUMBER NECKLACES

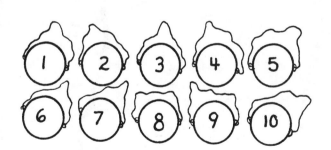

Make number necklaces for the children to wear while you sing "One, Two, Buckle My Shoe." The children stand when they hear the number they are wearing.

SOUND

Vv — Velveteen Rabbit

Read the book, *"The Velveteen Rabbit"* to your class. Have the children bring in some of their "real" toys to share with their classmates.

Vv — Vanilla / Vegetables

Have vanilla pudding or vanilla ice cream for a special snack. Talk about the vegetables you eat with lunch each day.

Jj — Jump Ropes

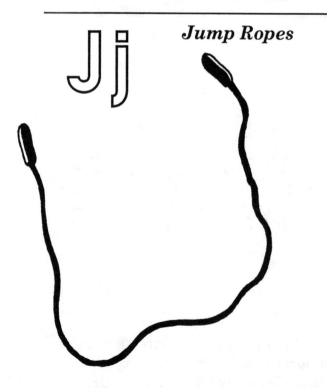

Have a jump rope contest to see who can jump the most times.

Jj — Jelly Beans and Jello

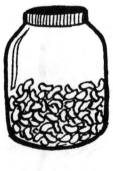

Have a jelly bean jar in the classroom to use as an *occasional* reward for particularly good behavior.

Make jello or jello squares.

LIBRARY

The Very Bumpy Bus Ride	by Michaela Muntean
The First Day Of School	by Marjorie Thayer
We Laughed A Lot, My First Day At School	by Sylvia Root Tester
Shawn Goes To School	by Petronella Breinburg
All Ready For School	by Leone Adleman

MUSIC

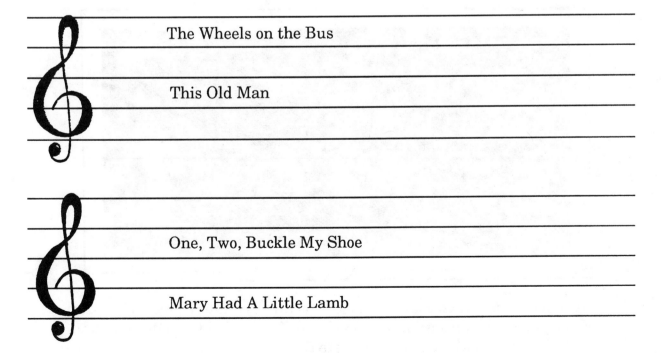

The Wheels on the Bus

This Old Man

One, Two, Buckle My Shoe

Mary Had A Little Lamb

ART

COLORED GLUE PICTURES

Make ordinary white glue fun by putting a few drops of food coloring in the bottle and shaking it until you have colored glue. Make three or four different colors and let the children draw pictures by squeezing the colored glue onto pieces of white paper. The colors will remain when the glue becomes hard and dries.

BLACK BOARD PICTURES

Have your students create a chalkboard picture by gluing a piece of black construction paper onto an outline of a chalkboard frame. Let them draw a picture with chalk on the black paper to complete the project. Spray with hairspray to preserve.

ART

BULLETIN BOARDS FOR KIDS

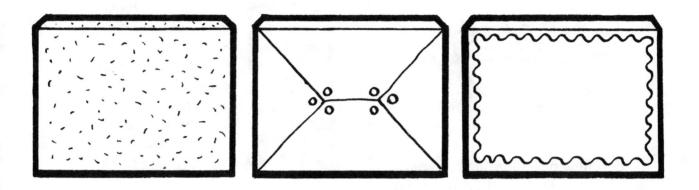

Make inexpensive bulletin boards using styrofoam sheets, fabric, thumb tacks and ribbon or braid. Cover a thin piece of styrofoam with a piece of fabric large enough to cover the front and back of the styrofoam. Secure in the back with thumb tacks. Decorate the front by gluing ribbon or braid close to the edge. Each child will have his or her own bulletin board to take home.

SCHOOL BUS

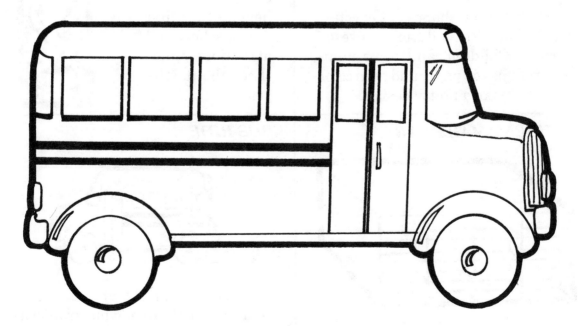

Enlarge this school bus pattern for each child. After the children color the picture, they can cut out pictures of children's faces from magazines or catalogs and glue in the windows.

CLASS ACTIVITIES

BOBBING FOR APPLES

Bob for apples just before snack time, then allow the children to eat their apples for snack.

LEARNING TO LACE AND TIE

Punch holes in a shoe box lid and string a long shoelace through the holes. Children can learn to lace and tie on this special and easy-to-make board.

STENCILS

Cut common shapes out of coffee can lids for the children to use as stencils. Children can trace a number of shapes on paper and then color them to make a pretty design.

HEIGHT CHART

Purchase or make a height chart to hang on the classroom wall or door. Record student's height the first day of school and at various times throughout the year.

STUDENT MAILBOXES

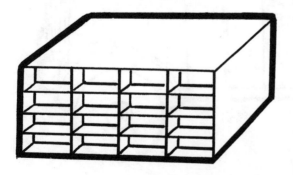

Purchase cardboard shoe storage boxes to use as mailboxes for your students.

BUS RIDE

Most preschools and day care centers do not provide bus transportation. If possible arrange to take your class for a ride on a school bus or even a public city bus.

October

CALENDAR

Sunday	Monday	Tuesday	Wednesday	Thursday	Friday	Saturday
			1	2	3	4
5	6	7	8	9	10	11
12	13	14	15	16	17	18
19	20	21				

Enlarge this squirrel pattern on gray or brown construction paper for your October calendar. Then reproduce the acorn pattern below on brown paper and number from 1 to 31.

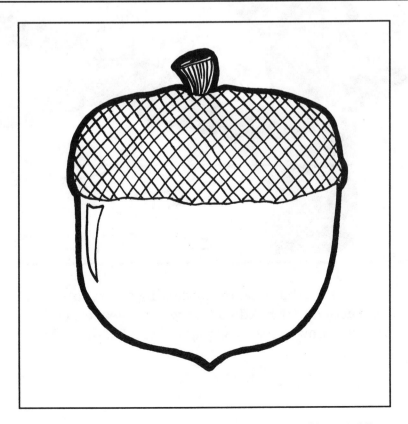

OCTOBER
BULLETIN BOARDS

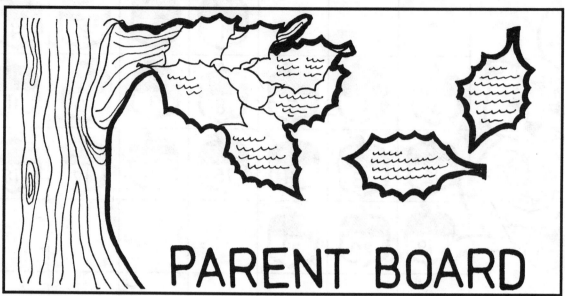

PARENT BOARD

Begin this month's Parent Board by cutting a large brown tree out of construction paper. Then use the leaf pattern included on page 23 to cut out a number of fall-colored leaves. Cut out a few extra leaves to write the Parent Board information on.

BIRTHDAY BOARD

Begin this month's Birthday Board by cutting a very large orange or yellow moon out of construction paper. Add a tree without leaves, cut out of black construction paper. Use the owl pattern on page 35 to label the children's names and birthdates.

LEAF PATTERN FOR THE PARENT BOARD

Directions are found on page 22.

WINDOW SCENE

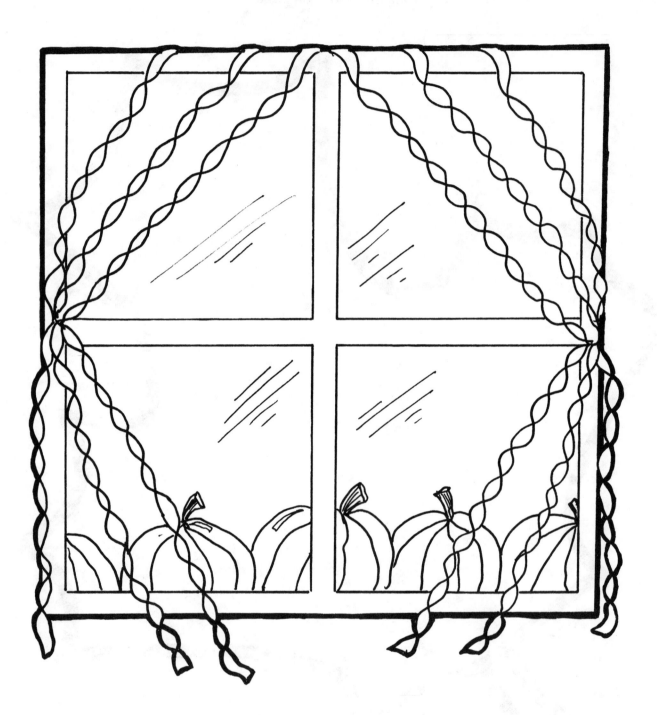

Hang alternating strands of green and orange streamers from your window creating the look of curtains. Make a pumpkin patch at the bottom by adding construction paper pumpkins with stems and leaves.

CUBBY LABEL

Acorn

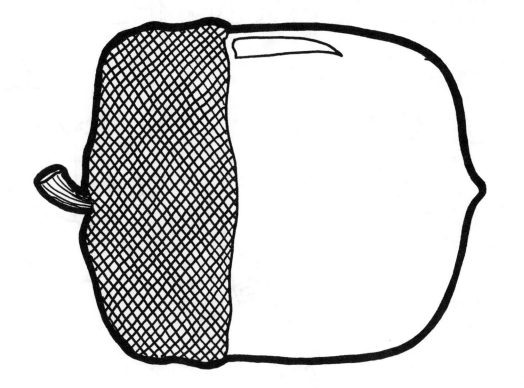

TABLE LABEL

Apple

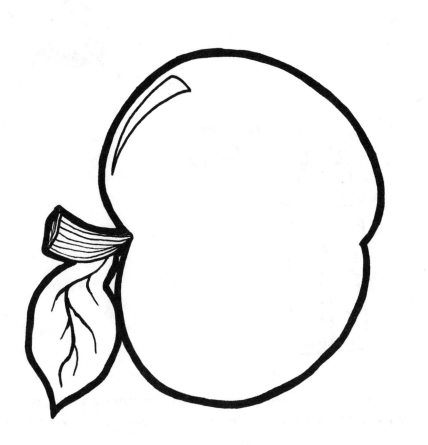

Plans and Patterns for Preschool

T.S. Denison & Co., Inc.

DRAMATIC PLAY

Place a number of career costumes in your Dramatic Play area this month.
If possible, try to include some of the props or "tools" each career might use.

SCIENCE

BOOK OF LEAVES

Collect leaves that have fallen outdoors and then allow each child to glue them onto paper, creating a "Book Of Leaves."

SORTING LEAVES

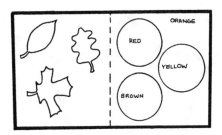

On a large orange piece of paper or poster board, create a game board like the one above *(omitting the color words)*. Have an envelope full of leaves made of various colors and shapes. Children can sort them according to shape on the left side of the board and according to color on the right side of the board.

(leaf patterns on the following page)

SORTING REAL NUTS

Label margarine tubs or small bowls with pictures of different kinds of nuts. Have real nuts available for children to sort into the correct bowls.

Discuss Halloween Safety Rules:

1. Don't go Trick or Treating alone or just with children. Have an adult go with you.

2. Only go to the homes of people you know.

3. Don't eat any of the candy until your parents have checked it.

4. Always walk on the sidewalks rather than on the road.

5. Always wear some light clothing or reflector tape to keep yourself visible at night.

LEAF PATTERNS

To accompany the Leaf Sorting Game found on page 27 - Science Activities

MATH

PUMPKIN PATCH SCENES

Make 10 pumpkin patch scenes such as the one above. Each one should have circles drawn on the scene where the children will place candy pumpkins *(or construction paper pumpkins)*. Number the circles from 1 to 10. For example, the pumpkin patch scene above has circles numbered from 1 to 6. A child would place 6 pumpkins in this pumpkin patch.

FENCE SCENES

Using dark blue paper, make ten night time fence scenes with bright yellow moons in the corner, labeled with a number between 1 and 10. Have cut-outs of black cats available for children to place on each fence, according to the number on that fence scene.

LEAF PUZZLE

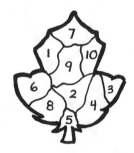 

This puzzle activitiy can be reproduced for each child or kept as a Math Center game. Reproduce the two pages of leaf patterns *(pages 30 & 31)*. Cut one of the leaves out and then cut the puzzle pieces apart. Children will either put the number on top of the correct number of dots or put the dot pieces on top of the correct number.

SQUIRREL & NUT GAME

Reproduce the squirrel and nut patterns 10 times. *(Patterns found on page 32.)* Write a number between 1 and 10 on each tree. Have real nuts or brown paper circles available for children to place on the hole according to the number on the tree.

LEAF PUZZLE PATTERN

Directions found on page 29.

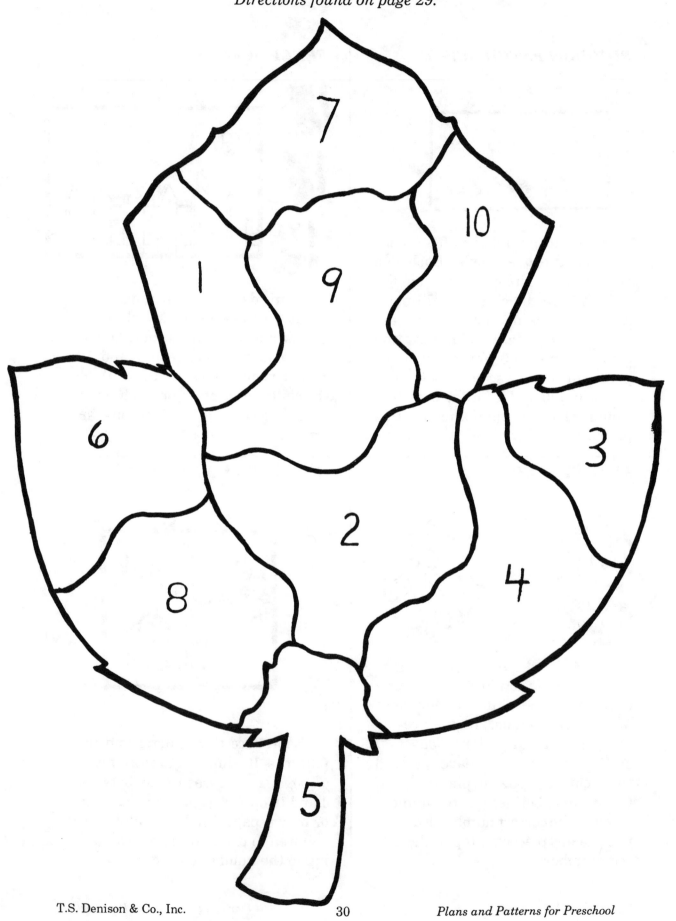

LEAF PUZZLE PATTERN

Directions found on page 29.

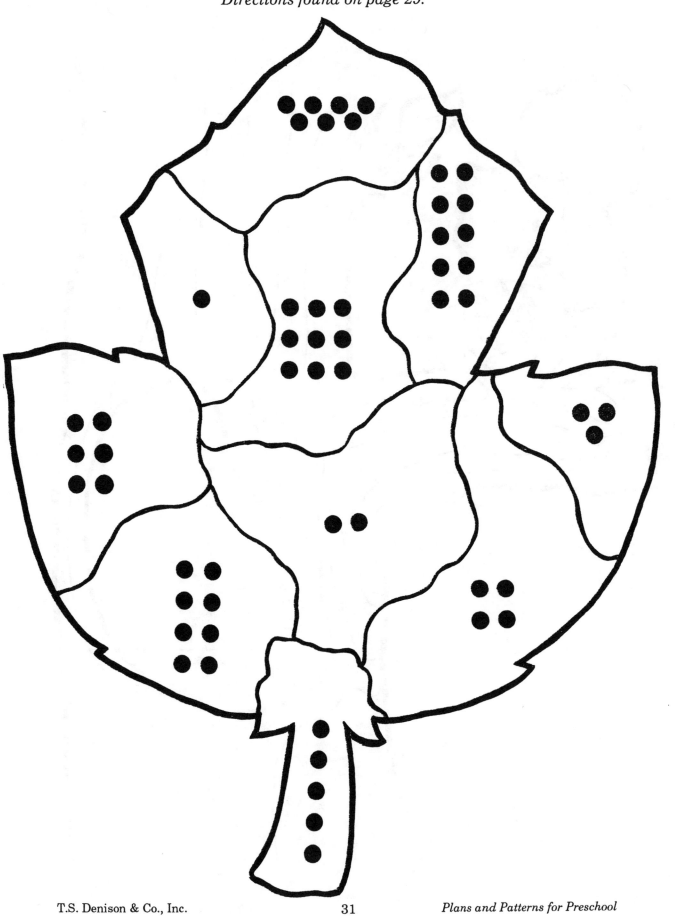

SQUIRREL AND NUTS NUMBER GAME

Directions are found on page 29.

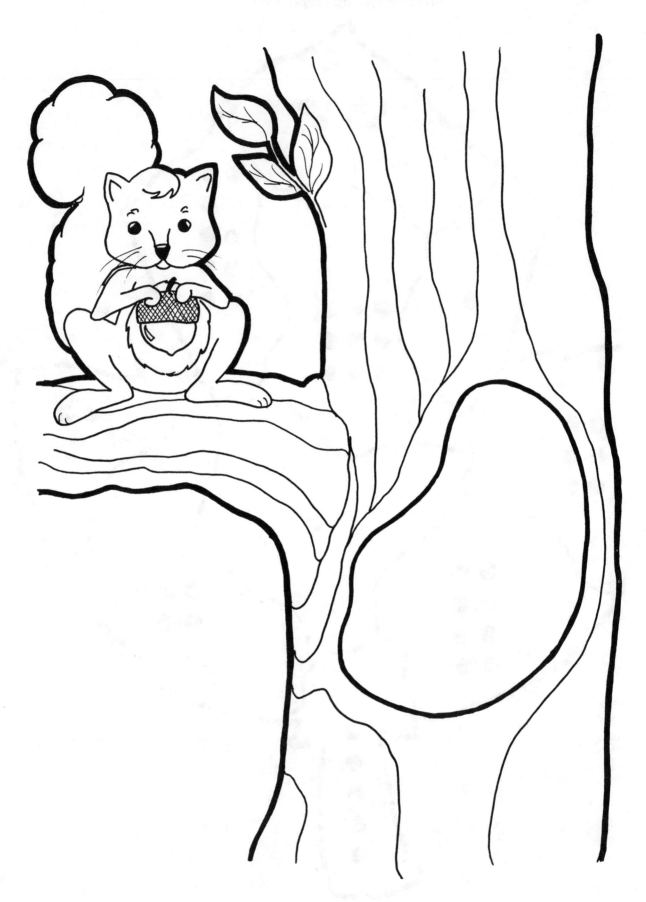

SOUND

Dd — *Dolls*

Have a "Doll Day" on which your students are encouraged to bring a doll from home to show to the class. Encourage the boys to bring dolls as well as the girls. A stuffed animal could be substituted if necessary.

Dd — *Dominoes*

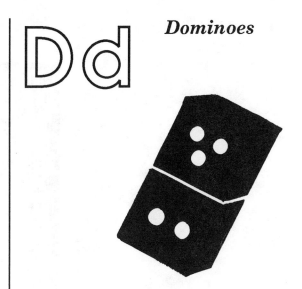

Have "Dominoes" set out on your sound table for students to experiment with. They can play with them in the traditional way or they can build creatively with them.

Xx — *Xylophone*

Begin by explaining that although xylophone begins with the letter "X", an "X" does not make the "Z" sound that you hear at the beginning of the word. Most children have a xylophone at home. Ask them to bring them to school and teach them how to play a simple song.

Xx — *X-Ray*

Bring a real X-ray to class for discussion and examination.

ART

NATURE PICTURES

Make Nature Pictures on poster board by gluing sticks around the edges to make a frame. Add leaves, small pebbles, and other "treasures" found outdoors.

LEAF CREATURES

Glue real leaves or leaf cut-outs onto pieces of colored construction paper. Children add faces, hands and feet to create "Leaf Creatures."

ART

LEAF RUBBINGS

Have the children collect fallen leaves outdoors. Then place the leaves under a thin piece of white paper. Rub over the leaves with the side of a crayon until a picture of the leaf appears.

BIRTHDAY BOARD OWL

Use the patterns found on page 36, to make this owl. When finished, write the student's name and birthdate on the back with a black marker and put them on the Birthday Board. Children who do not have October birthdays will also enjoy making this darling owl.

BIRTHDAY BOARD OWL PATTERNS

Directions are found on page 35.

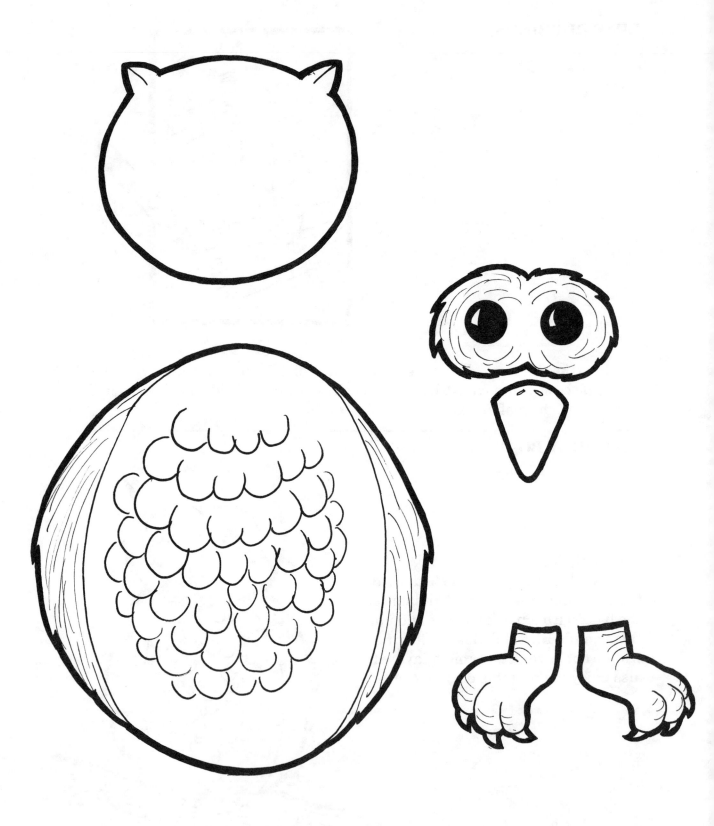

LIBRARY

In Fall	by Rochelle Nielson-Barshun, Jane Belk Moncure and Elenor Hammond
Our Halloween Book	by Jane Belk Moncure
Fall Is Here	by Jane Belk Moncure
Georgie's Halloween	by Robert Bright
Trick or Treat	by Louis Slobodkin
Autumn Story	by Jill Barklem
All For Fall	by Ethel and Leonard Kessler

MUSIC

London Bridge

The Mail Must Go Through

Twinkle, Twinkle, Little Star

CLASS ACTIVITIES

RAKING LEAVES

Rake leaves on your center's playground or at your local park. Allow the children to jump and play in the piles of leaves. *(You may need to rerake and bag the leaves when you are done.)*

APPLE CRISP

Make apple crisp for a warm tasty snack on a cool fall day.

You Will Need: 4-6 sliced apples; 1/2 cup sugar; 2 tbls. butter; 1 egg; 1 cup flour; 2 tsp. baking powder; 1/4 tsp salt.

What you do: Fill greased 9" x 9" pan 2/3 full of sliced apples. Sprinkle with sugar and dot with butter. Mix listed ingredients and put on top of apples. Bake at 350° for 40 minutes. Makes 9-12 servings.

PUMPKIN BARS

Carve a pumpkin and use the pulp to make Pumpkin Bars. The recipe is included on page 44.

FIELD TRIP TO A PUMPKIN PATCH

Take a field trip to a pumpkin patch and purchase pumpkins and other fall produce to use in making a display for your classroom or center's entry way.

TELL THE STORY OF LITTLE BEAR'S STAR

Tell the story about the little bear who goes in search of a house with no windows or doors, a chimney on top and a star in the middle. Little bear finally finds the house when he cuts an apple open crosswide and sees the star!

You will of course, need to bring a red apple and a knife to school to show the children that an apple really does have a star in the midddle.

THE APPLE ORCHARD

If possible, take your students on a field trip to an Apple Orchard or arrange to take them on an old-fashioned hay ride!

EXTRA FUN HALLOWEEN IDEAS AND PROJECTS

BLACK BAT

Use this pattern to cut out a black bat out of construction paper for each child. Mark lines with a pencil for the eyes and mouth. Children can put on their own glue and then add silver glitter. Hang from the ceiling to decorate your classroom.

SPIDER

Make spiders out of 4" styrofoam balls which have been spray painted black.
The children can give their spiders legs by inserting 8 pipe cleaners into the ball.
Glue on small construction paper eyes and a mouth.

PUMPKIN COOKIES

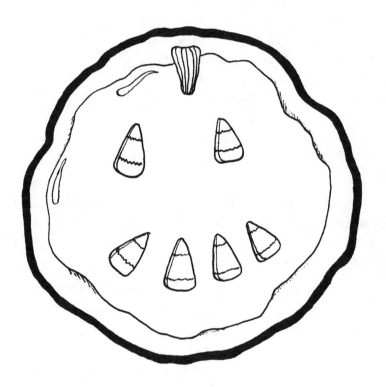

Purchase ready-to-bake sugar cookie dough at the store and bake round "pumpkin-shaped" cookies. Allow the children to frost them with orange frosting and decorate with candy corn. These can be used as a special treat at your Halloween party.

PUMPKIN BAR RECIPE

Batter:
    1 cup oil
    4 eggs
    2 cups pumpkin
    2 tsp. cinnamon
    2 cups sugar
    1/2 tsp. salt
    1 tsp. soda
    2 tsp. baking powder
    2 cups unsifted flour

Combine oil and sugar; beat until well-blended. Add eggs one at a time, beating at least 45 seconds after each one. Add pumpkins; beat till blended. Add remaining ingredients. Pour into greased cookie sheet or jelly roll (10" x 16") pan. Bake at 350° degrees for 25 - 30 minutes.

NOVEMBER

"THANKSGIVING"

November

Sunday	Monday	Tuesday	Wednesday	Thursday	Friday	Saturday
				1	2	3
4	5	6	7	8	9	10
11	12	13	14			

Make a very large cornucopia out of light brown construction paper *(cornucopia pattern is found on page 58.)* Then reproduce the food patterns included on the following pages. Color them and number from 1 to 30.

CALENDAR PATTERNS

CALENDAR PATTERNS

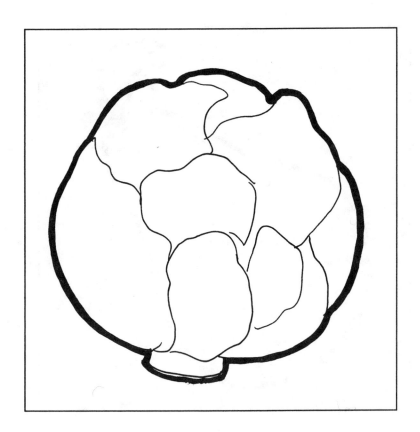

CALENDAR PATTERNS

NOVEMBER
BULLETIN BOARDS

PARENT BOARD

Cut out a turkey shape from brown construction paper to begin this November Parent Board. Add a border of feathers.

BIRTHDAY BOARD

Enlarge the boy and girl patterns for this November Birthday Board. Write the children's names and birthdates on the feathers.

WINDOW SCENE

Put alternating pieces of brown and orange construction paper around all four edges of your window for a border. On page 64 is the art project "Tee-pees." Have the children make the tee-pees and then put them on display in your "Indian Village" window scene.

When you create this scene in your classroom, be sure to provide the children with factual information about Indian people. Not all Indians lived in tee-pees. Show the children pictures of a variety of homes that Indian people lived in long ago. Then show the children pictures of how Indians live today, in cities, in rural areas. Show pictures of some of the beautiful art work that is created by the Indian People.

CUBBY LABEL
Pilgrim Hat

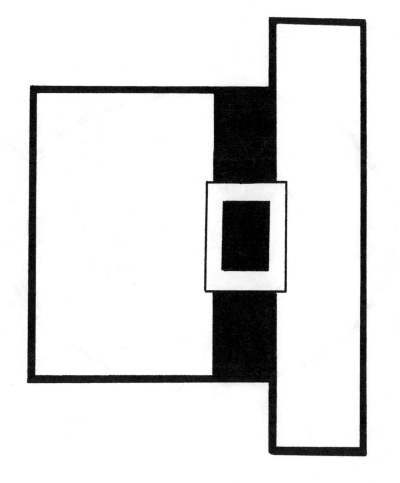

TABLE LABEL
Pilgrim

Plans and Patterns for Preschool

T.S. Denison & Co., Inc.

CUBBY LABEL
Pilgrim Hat

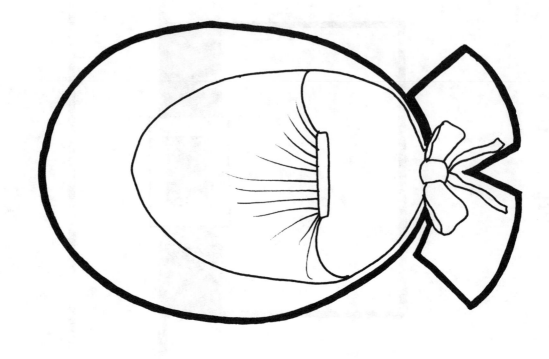

Plans and Patterns for Preschool

TABLE LABEL
Pilgrim

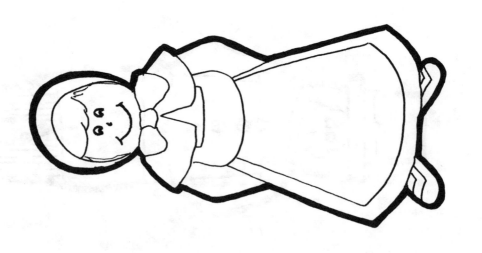

T.S. Denison & Co., Inc.

DRAMATIC PLAY

Let your students pretend to be present at the very first Thanksgiving dinner that the Pilgrims attended. You will need a table complete with plates, cups, silverware, Pilgrim hats and Indian head pieces, a large kettle and plastic food for them to "cook."

SCIENCE

POTATOES

Give each student a jar which is 3/4 full of water, a potato and 3 or 4 toothpicks. Put the potato in the top of the jar so that the bottom 1" or so is in the water. If the potato is small enough to fall through into the jar, put the toothpicks in the sides to hold it up. Keep enough water in the jar to keep the end of the potato wet. Pretty soon roots will grow from the bottom and sprouts from the sides.

TURKEYS

Everyone talks about turkeys at Thanksgiving time. Teach your children about real turkeys with a library book or encyclopedia. They may be surprised to find out that they look quite different than the colorful pictures they are used to.

FEATHERS

Bring a variety of feathers to class for the children to examine. Discuss how feathers were once used as ink pens and how they are used for pillows and coat or quilt stuffing today.

THANKSGIVING COSTUME PICTURES

Have your students become aware of their size and body shape by having them lie down on very large pieces of paper. Trace around each of the children. Have the children color their picture to look like themselves, possibly wearing a Pilgrim or Indian costume.

MATH

COUNTING FEATHERS

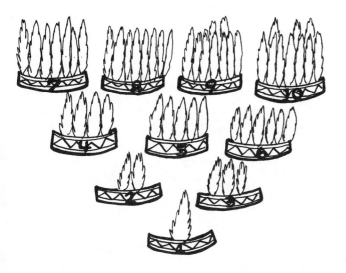

Have your students make Indian head bands, numbering them from 1 to 10 and placing the corresponding number of feathers in each.

CORNUCOPIA

Reproduce and color 10 of the cornucopia patterns, found on page 58. Lable each with a number between 1 and 10. Reproduce and color food patterns, found on pages 47 to 50 (*the food calendar patterns*). Children place the appropriate number of foods on each cornucopia.

THE MAYFLOWER

Reproduce 10 copies of the Mayflower pattern, found on page 59. Number the ships from 1 to 10. Also make multiple copies of the Pilgrim patterns, found on page 60, on black construction paper. Children place the correct number of Pilgrims with each ship.

PILGRIM DOT-TO-DOT

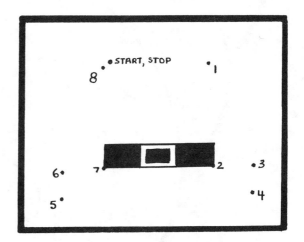

Reproduce a copy of the Pilgrim Dot-To-Dot, found on page 61. The children connect the dots and color the hat.

CORNUCOPIA

Directions found on page 57.

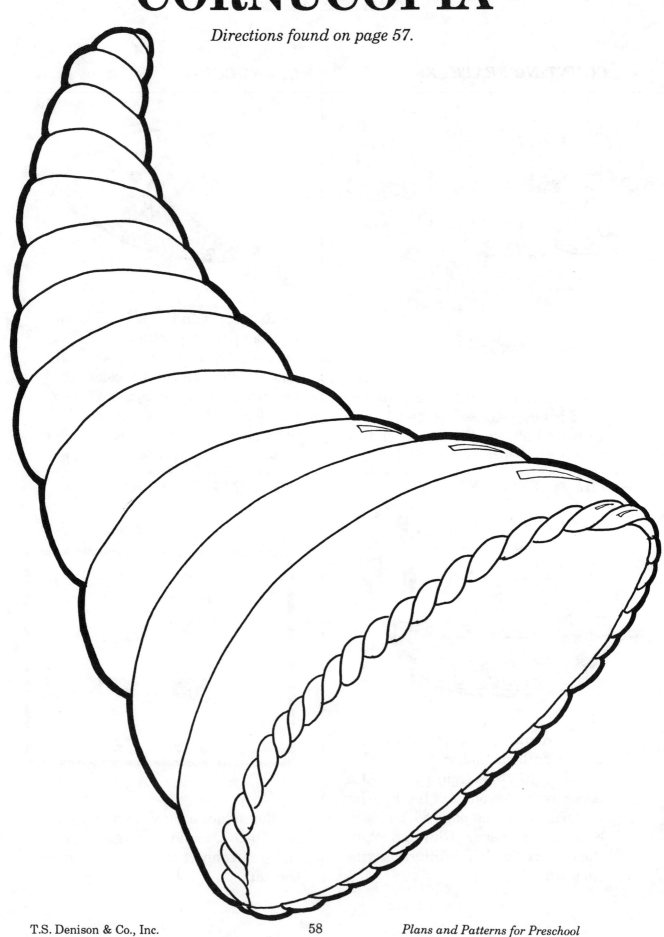

THE MAYFLOWER

Directions found on page 57.

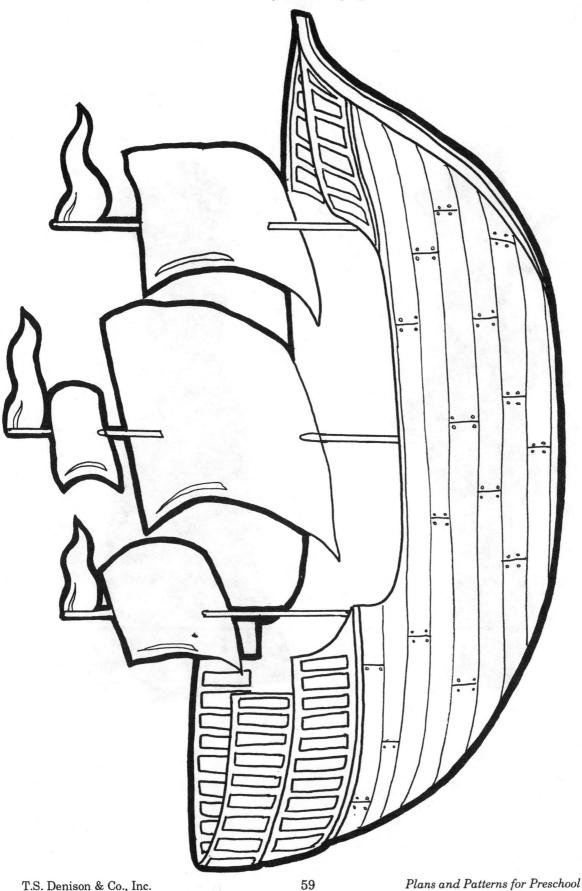

PILGRIM PATTERNS

To accompany "The Mayflower Math Game," found on page 57.

PILGRIM DOT-TO-DOT

Directions found on page 57.

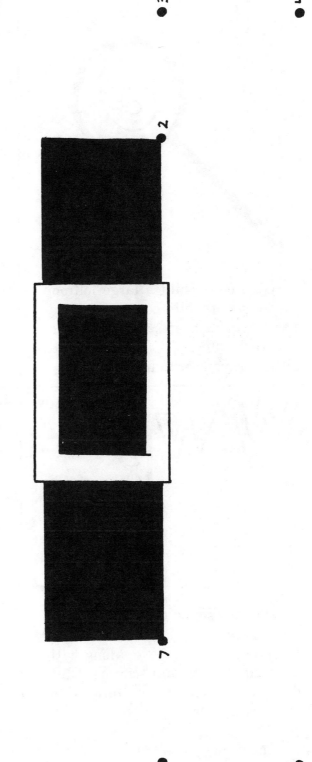

SOUND

L l   *Lollipop*

Give each child a large lollipop made out of white construction paper or poster board. Children decorate their lollipops as they wish with either crayons or markers.

L l   *Letter*

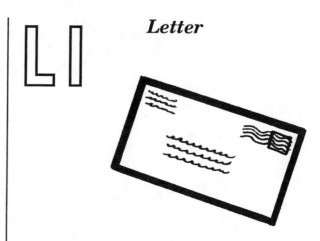

Help your students to write a letter of "Thanks" to their parents during the Thanksgiving season. Obtain their home addresses with the cooperation of the parents and allow the children to actually mail the letters to their homes. *(Ask each parent to donate a stamp!)*

W w   *Wish Bones*

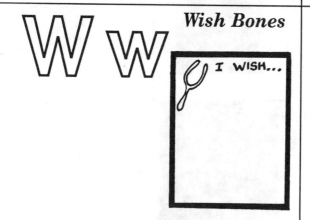

I WISH...

On your sound table this month, have a stack of paper available like the one pictured above, along with magazines, glue and scissors. Children cut out pictures of things they are wishing for.

Encourage unselfish wishes and encourage wishes for friends and family members.

W w   *Wood*

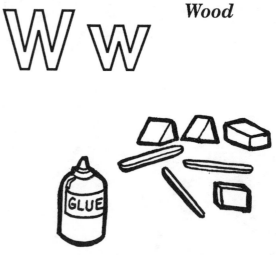

GLUE

Purchase a bag or two of small wood scraps and popsicle sticks at a craft store. Allow the children to be creative and glue the pieces together to make whatever they wish.

ART

CANDY CORN TURKEYS

Reproduce this turkey pattern, then trace it onto a piece of heavy white paper for each child. Have them color the turkey and then glue on candy corn feathers.

INDIAN HEADDRESS

Give each student a paper strip 2" wide and long enough to wrap around his or her head leaving an inch or two extra for overlap. Allow the children to decorate the band as they wish. Fit the band to the child's head and tape together. Add three to five feathers.

ART

INDIAN VESTS

Make Indian Vests out of brown paper grocery bags. Begin by cutting a slit from the top of the bag to the bottom continuing to cut about an inch into the bottom of the bag and cutting out a circle large enough to fit around a child's neck. This will be the top of the vest.

Next, cut armholes out of the sides of the bags. Cut slits on the bottom to make fringe if you wish. Allow the children to decorate the Indian Vests with crayons or colored chalk.

TRIANGLE-SHAPED TEE-PEE

Cut out a triangle-shaped tee-pee for each child using brown construction paper or grocery bags. Allow the children to decorate them as they wish. Hang the tee-pees in the window to make an Indian Village Scene.

LIBRARY

Julian In The Autumn Woods	by Milena Lukesova`
Our Thanksgiving Book	by Jane Belk Moncure
Sometimes It's Turkey - Sometimes It's Feathers	by Lorna Balian
Jimmy And Joe Have A Real Thanksgiving	by Sally Glendinning
Best Thanksgiving Book	by Pat Whitehead
Why We Have Thanksgiving	by Margaret Hillet

MUSIC

 Ten Little Indians

The Bear Went Over The Mountain

 Shortnin' Bread

CLASS ACTIVITIES

PUMPKIN SEEDS

Buy a pumpkin to carve as you did in October. This time, save the seeds. Wash them twice in cool water and allow to dry. Place the seeds in a single layer on a cookie sheet, then sprinkle with melted butter. Finally, salt the seeds and bake at 300° for 15 to 25 minutes or until slightly browned.

THANKSGIVING LUNCHEON

Invite your student's parents to a special Thanksgiving luncheon. Have the children prepare as much of the meal as possible.

PUMPKIN PIE

Make a pumpkin pie to use as dessert at your Thanksgiving luncheon.

Recipe is found on page 67.

SWEETCORN

Buy a dozen ears of sweetcorn, still in their husks at a grocery store or produce stand. Let the children husk the corn and clean it themselves. Cook it for lunch and serve with melted butter and salt.

POPCORN

Pop popcorn in a pan on the stove. This is closer to the way the Indians did it than the modern popcorn poppers or microwave popcorn.

CORNMEAL BREAD

You will need: 1/4 cup melted shortening; 1 tbls. salt; 2 beaten eggs; 1/2 cup sugar; 1 1/2 cups cornmeal; 6 1/2 cups flour; 1 pkg. yeast; 1/4 cup warm water; 2 cups warm milk; 1/4 cup melted butter.

Dissolve yeast in 1/4 cup warm water and set aside for ten minutes; add remaining ingredients. Mix well and let rise until double in size. Punch down and shape into loaves. Place in greased loaf pans and let rise again until double. Bake at 375° for 45 minutes.

PUMPKIN PIE RECIPE

In a sauce pan combine:

1/3 cup brown sugar
1 envelope Knox Gelatin
1/4 tsp. salt
1 tsp. cinnamon
1/4 tsp. nutmeg
1/4 tsp. ginger

Into this mixture combine:

3 egg yolks
1/2 cup milk

Cook over medium heat, stirring constantly until boiling. Remove from heat and stir in one cup of canned pumpkin pie filling. Chill one hour.

Beat three egg whites until soft peaks form. Gradually beat in 1/4 cup sugar to form stiff peaks. Fold pumpkin mixture into it. Turn into graham cracker crust and chill 2 to 3 hours before serving.

DECEMBER

December CALENDAR

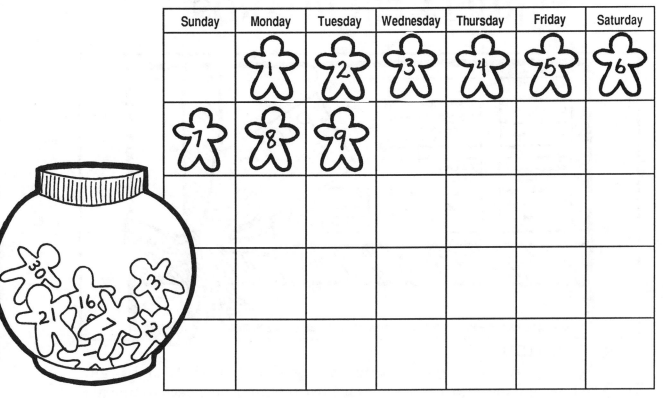

Sunday	Monday	Tuesday	Wednesday	Thursday	Friday	Saturday
	1	2	3	4	5	6
7	8	9				

Make a very large cookie jar out of white construction paper. Tie a real red or green ribbon at the top. Reproduce the Gingerbread Man pattern below 39 times; 31 for numbers with 8 extra for "DECEMBER." Reproduce on light brown paper and decorate with markers.

DECEMBER
BULLETIN BOARDS

PARENT BOARD

Make your December Parent Board into a large Christmas or Hanukkah gift. Use a red background with a green bow for Christmas or a blue background and a silver bow for Hanukkah. Then add the Parent Board heading on a large white gift tag.

BIRTHDAY BOARD

Make a seasonal Birthday board by reproducing the bell pattern *(on the following page)* and stringing them across the board. Label them with the children's names and birthdates. Add musical notes and a BIRTHDAY BELLS heading.

BELL PATTERN
FOR THE BIRTHDAY BOARD

WINDOW SCENE

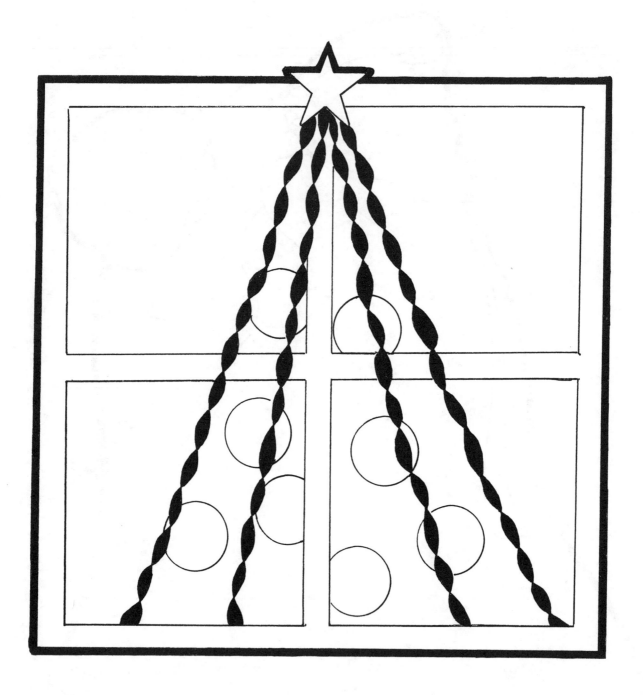

Cut a large circle out of colored paper for each child and let them decorate the circles as Christmas tree ornaments using glitter, ribbon and small pieces of construction paper. Hang these ornaments on the window first. Then hang green crepe paper streamers in the shape of a Christmas tree. Add a star or an angel on the top and presents at the bottom if you wish.

CUBBY LABEL
Candy Cane

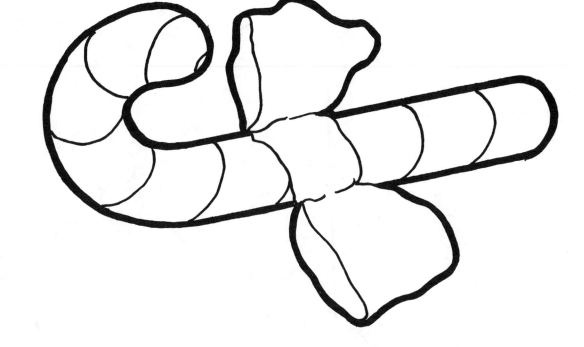

TABLE LABEL
Stocking

Plans and Patterns for Preschool

T.S. Denison & Co., Inc.

DRAMATIC PLAY

Create a snow scene on your walls with a construction paper house, trees and mailbox. Use either white paint or canned snow to put snow on the housetop and tops of the trees, as well as hills of snow. Have a table in this area where children can write letters to Santa Claus or cut out pictures of toys they want from catalogs. Include paper, pencils, envelopes, catalogs, scissors and glue.

SCIENCE

HIDDEN SMELL JARS

Make "hidden smell" jars like you did in September. When you make them this time use only scents that are familiar to the Christmas Season such as evergreen, ginger, mint and candles.

CHRISTMAS PLANTS

Keep different Christmas plants on your science table during the month of December for the children to examine. Examples would include holly, pointsettias, mistletoe and Christmas cactus.

PINE TREE NEEDLES

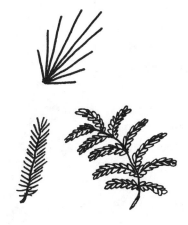

Explain that Christmas trees have needles instead of leaves. Show the children samples of the various kinds of needles that are found on Christmas trees. Ask the children to bring a small sample of their Christmas tree.

THE NORTH POLE

Almost all children have heard about the North Pole but probably do not know exactly where the North Pole is located. Bring in a children's encyclopedia to your class to help you explain it to the children.

MATH

PAPER CHAIN CALENDAR

At the beginning of December, make a paper chain of 25 links and hang it from the ceiling. Each morning take off one link and count how many are left. Children will be able to see how fast the holiday season is approaching.

CANDLE PUZZLE

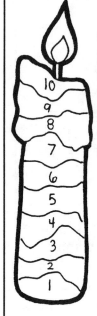

Use the candle pattern on page 79 to make a puzzle for each child. Cut the pieces apart, color them and put them in numerical order to make the candle. Put a flame on the top to complete the puzzle.

CHRISTMAS STOCKINGS

Use the patterns included on page 80 to make 10 Christmas stockings and small presents. Children place the correct number of candies, toys and presents with each stocking.

PRESENTS

Use the patterns included on page 81 to make 10 Christmas presents of progressive sizes and numbers. Children place them on the correct places on the Christmas tree picture page.

CANDLE PUZZLE

Directions found on page 78.

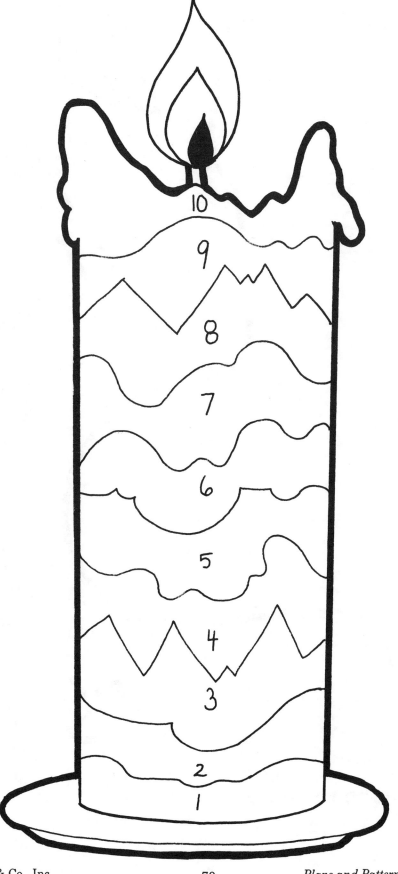

CHRISTMAS STOCKINGS

Directions found on page 78.

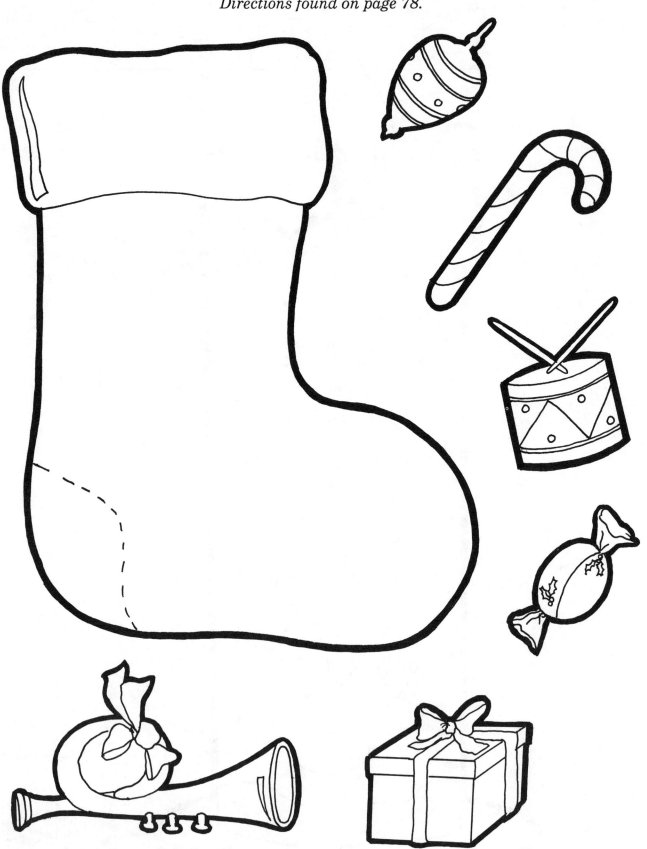

PRESENTS

Directions found on page 78.

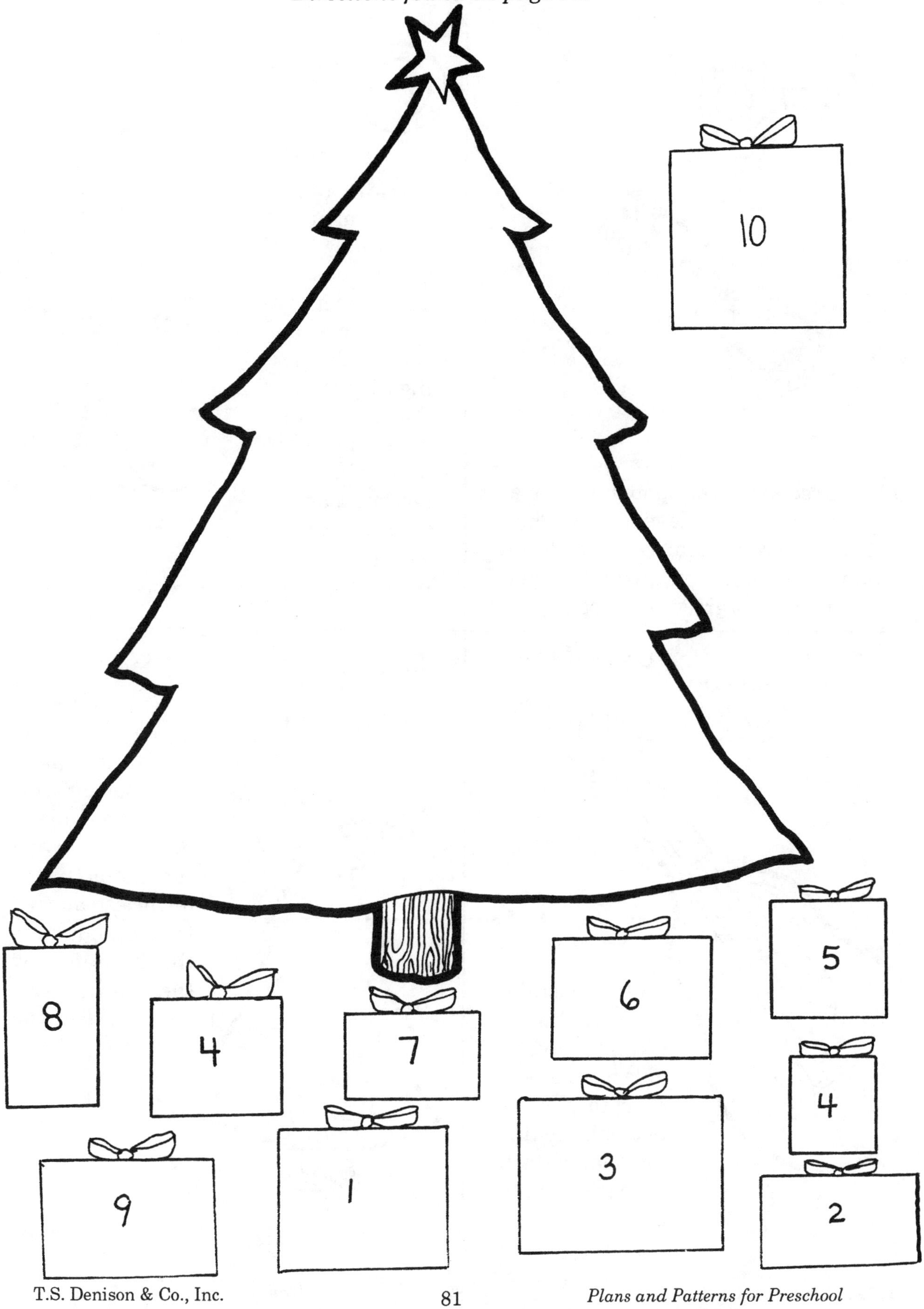

10

8

4

7

6

5

9

1

3

4

2

SOUND

Green

Green is a very popular color at Christmas time. Have a "green day" on which you encourage the children to wear green, serve green foods and color or paint green pictures.

Gingerbread

Have ginger-bread men cut out of light brown construction paper sitting on your sound table during the month of December. Provide the children with crayons and markers to decorate the gingerbread men.

Ukulele

If possible, have a real or toy ukulele available for the children to play. If not, enlarge this ukulele pattern for each child to color.

Under

Children know that Christmas presents belong "under" the Christmas tree. Give them a picture of a Christmas tree to color, but have the children draw their own presents "under" the tree.

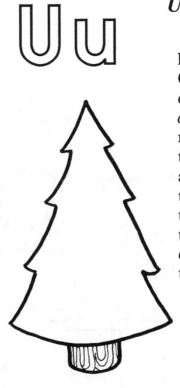

LIBRARY

The Night Before Christmas	by Clement C. Moore
Our Christmas Book	by Jane Belk Moncure
The Christmas Doll	by Wendy Mathis Parker
Grandpa Bear's Christmas	by Bonnie Pryor
My First Christmas Book	by Colleen L. Reece
The Polar Express	by Chris Van Allsburg
The Christmas Day Kitten	by James Herriot

MUSIC

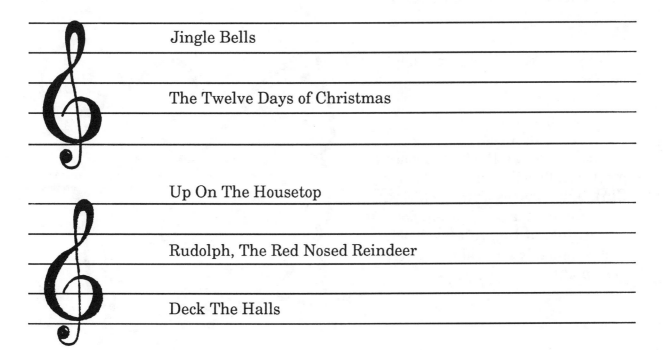

Jingle Bells

The Twelve Days of Christmas

Up On The Housetop

Rudolph, The Red Nosed Reindeer

Deck The Halls

ART

HOLLY WREATH

Give each child a paper plate with the inside circle already cut-out. Children glue green paper, cut in the shape of holly leaves to cover the paper ring. Then add red paper berries or small red cinnamon candies and a real or paper bow.

BAKING CLAY ORNAMENTS

Make Baking Clay by mixing together:
  4 cups of flour
  1 cup of salt
  1 cup of water
Roll dough 1/4" thick with rolling pin, then allow the children to cut out Christmas shapes with cookie cutters. Bake in a 400° oven for 45 minutes or until lightly browned. Let cool completely and paint with tempera paints.

ART

LAMP POSTS

Use the pattern provided on page 86 to cut out the construction paper pieces needed to make the lamp posts. First, glue the yellow background behind the large opening, then glue on the large flame. If you wish, you may decorate the lamp post with a red ribbon or holly leaves and berries.

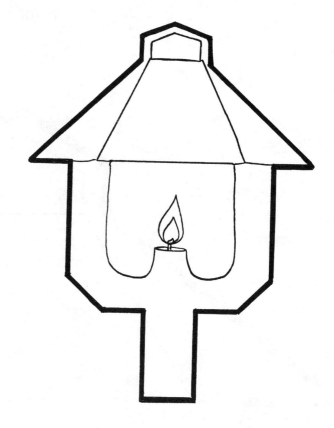

TRACING CHRISTMAS SHAPES

Give each child a large piece of lightly colored thin paper. The children trace Christmas shapes onto the paper with cookie cutters and then color. This paper can be used as wrapping paper for Christmas presents.

LAMP POST PATTERN

Directions found on page 85.

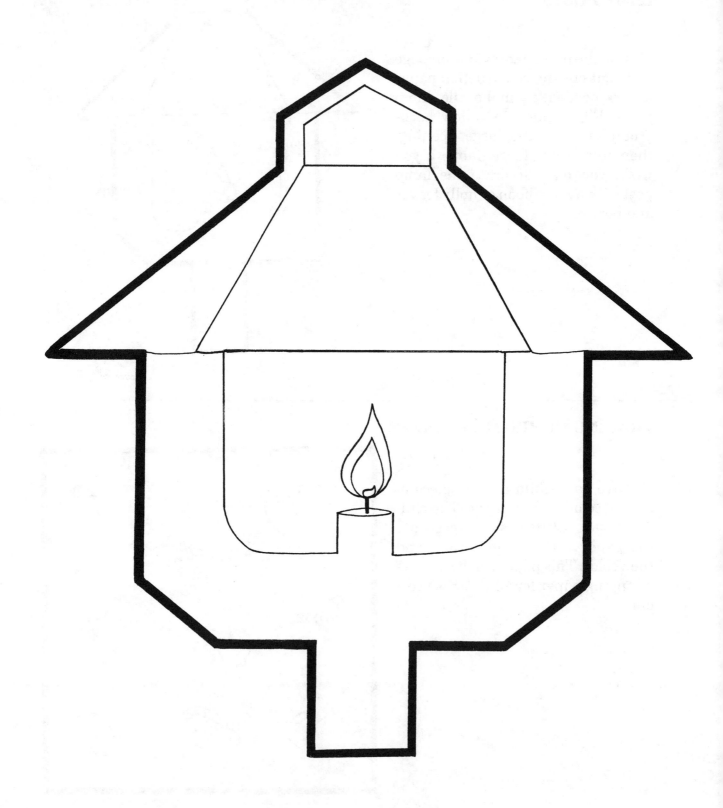

CLASS ACTIVITIES

BAKING GINGERBREAD MEN

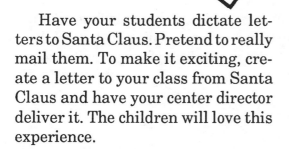

Bake and decorate gingerbread men.

The recipe is included on page 88.

POPCORN BALLS

Make popcorn balls:
    1½ cups white syrup
    2 tbls. butter
    ¼ tsp. baking soda
Boil syrup for 3 minutes. Add butter and baking soda. Pour over 4 quarts of popped corn. Wet hands with water and shape into balls.

LETTERS TO SANTA

Have your students dictate letters to Santa Claus. Pretend to really mail them. To make it exciting, create a letter to your class from Santa Claus and have your center director deliver it. The children will love this experience.

BAKE SALE

Hold a bake sale with the gingerbread men, popcorn balls and any other treats you might make.

GIFTS FOR THE KIDS

Use the money earned at the Bake Sale to buy presents or the craft material needed to make presents for children. Wrap them up in Christmas paper and bows.

SHARING AT CHRISTMAS TIME

Take the Christmas presents to a local Children's Home or Children's Hospital and give them to children who are unable to be with their families at Christmas time. Call ahead and offer to present a short play or sing some songs for the children.

GINGERBREAD MAN RECIPE

From the activity featured on page 87.

In medium bowl mix:
- 3 1/2 cups flour
- 2 tsp. ground ginger
- 1 tsp. cinnamon
- 1/2 tsp. salt
- 1/4 tsp. ground cloves

In large bowl mix:
- 1/3 cup softened butter
- 3/4 cup firmly packed brown sugar
- 2/3 cup molasses
- Alternately mix in flour mixture from the medium bowl and 1/3 cup water
- Stir in another cup of flour

Cover the mixture and chill at least 2 hours or until the dough is firm. Then on a lightly floured surface, roll dough 1/8" thick and cut with cookie cutters. Bake on a well-greased cookie sheet in a preheated 350° degree oven for approximately 15 minutes.

EXTRA FUN HANUKKAH IDEAS & PROJECTS

MENORAH

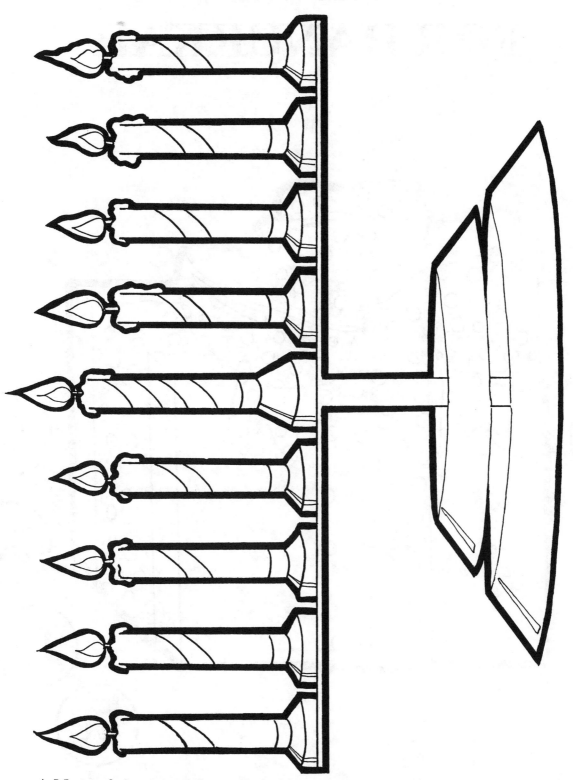

   A Menorah is a special candle holder which the Jewish People use during Hanukkah. The middle candle is used to light the other eight candles. One candle is lit for eight days. Using this pattern, cut a Menorah out of yellow construction paper for each child. Let the children glue on brown construction paper candles. Use gold glitter to make the flames above the candles.

GIFTS
FOR HANUKKAH

Wrap up small boxes with a few coins inside and give them to your students, explaining that children often receive coins and other gifts each day of the Hanukkah celebration.

A DREIDEL

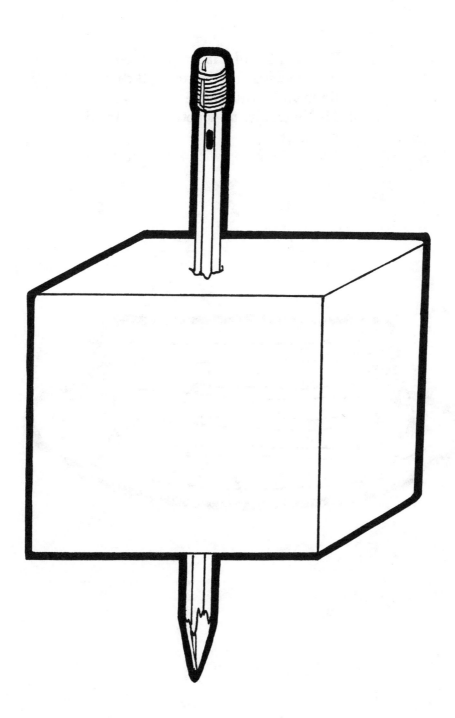

Give each child a styrofoam cube and a sharpened pencil. Help the children poke their pencil through the cube to make a dreidel, a special Hanukkah toy.

POTATO PANCAKES

1. Shred or grate 8 large potatoes.
2. Add one egg, 1/2 cup milk, 3 tbls.
   flour and a little salt.
3. Mix ingredients together and fry like
   pancakes.
4. Eat plain or top with syrup or sugar.

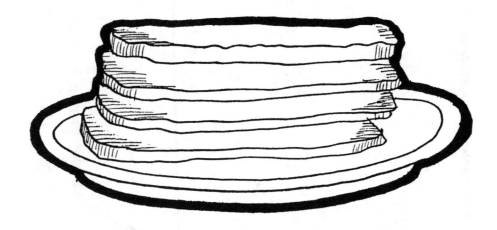

Using the above recipe, make potato pancakes, a traditional Hanukkah treat.

8 DAYS OF HANUKKAH

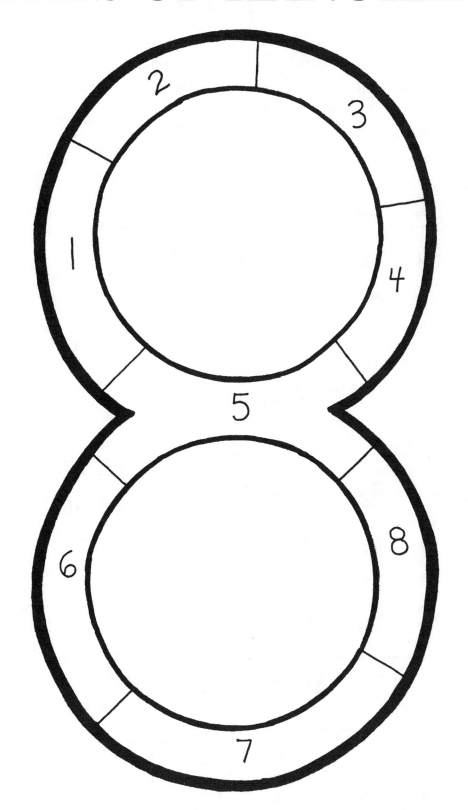

Explain to the children that Hanukkah is an eight day celebration. Have the children color in one section of this numeral 8 picture during each day of Hanukkah.

JANUARY

"WINTER WONDERLAND"

January

CALENDAR

Sunday	Monday	Tuesday	Wednesday	Thursday	Friday	Saturday
				1	2	3
4	5	6	7	8	9	10
11	12	13	14	15		

Enlarge pattern for mother penguin. Reproduce pattern for numbers. Color beak and feet orange and it's back black. Leave a white stomach.

Reproduce the small penguin for the numbers. Color the same as the mother penguin.

JANUARY
BULLETIN BOARDS

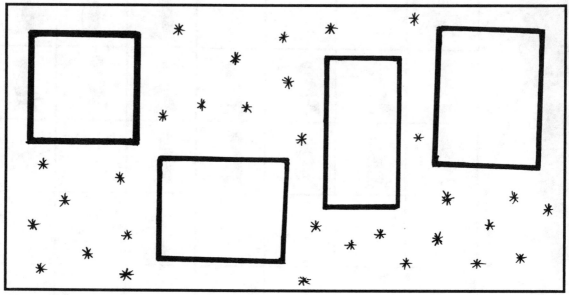

PARENT BOARD

Use a light blue background with white snowflakes around the edge for a border. Use the alphabet patterns provided on pages 108 to 121 to make the ice-capped letters for the Parent Board heading.

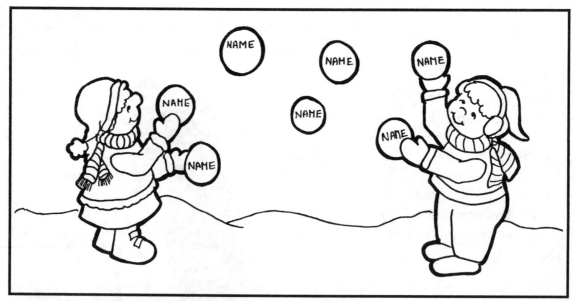

BIRTHDAY BOARD

Use light blue paper for the sky and white paper for the snow. Children may be enlarged and colored. Names and birthdates should be written on white snowballs. Make the heading letters out of white paper also.

WINDOW SCENE

Hang alternating strips of light blue and white crepe paper streamers. Twist them from the window top and pull them together at the center of each side and tape to the edge. If desired, bows can be made out of crepe paper and placed on top of the tape.

The snow can be made either by painting the window, using white contact paper or spraying canned snow on the window.

To make the window scene even more enjoyable, cut evergreen trees and a log cabin out of construction paper and tape to the window.

CUBBY LABEL
Hat

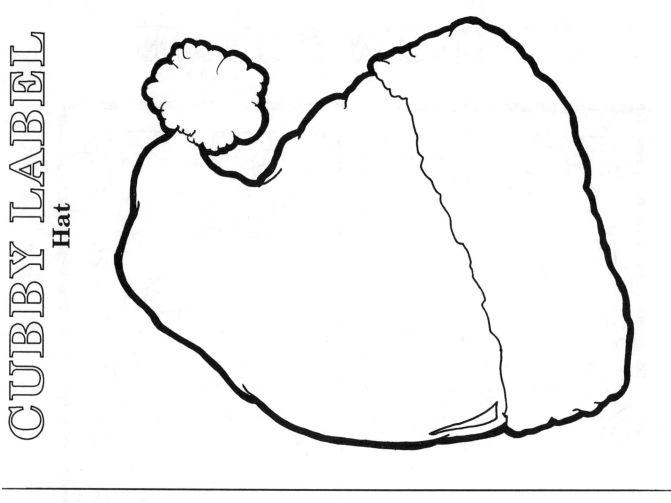

TABLE LABEL
Mitten

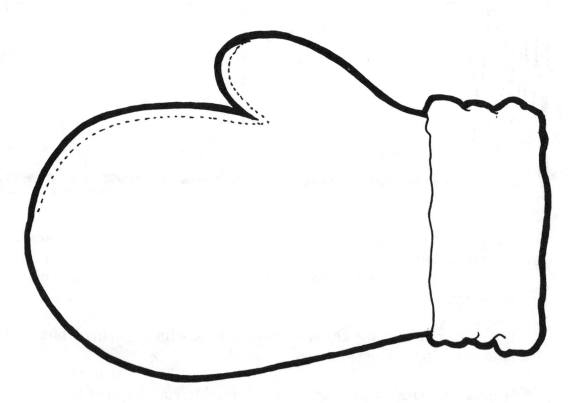

Plans and Patterns for Preschool

T.S. Denison & Co., Inc.

DRAMATIC PLAY

Use contact paper or construction paper to make the fireplace scene, book shelves, lamp, plants and wall hanging. Add rocking chair, hearth rug, blankets, books and sewing cards. Provide marshmallows and let the children pretend to roast them in the fireplace.

SCIENCE

CRYSTAL GARDEN

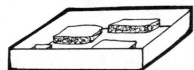

Grow a garden right in your classroom! Begin by placing five or six damp sponges in the bottom of a tin pie pan. Sprinkle the following over the sponges:

1. 4 tablespoons Bluing
2. 4 tablespoons salt
3. 1 tablespoon ammonia

A crystal garden will begin to grow over night.

(A garden like this is easily disturbed. Keep it in a safe place for viewing, not for touching!)

FORMS OF WATER

Examine the various forms of water. Start by placing ice cubes in a warm part of the classroom where they will melt fairly quickly. Then take the water and pour it into a pan which you can heat. Use a portable burner or a real stove if necessary and observe the steam as the water boils away.

THERMOMETERS

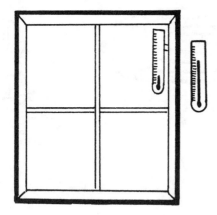

Place thermometers inside and outside of a classroom window. Read, record and compare temperatures at various times during the day all through the month of January.

MAKE YOUR OWN PLAY DOUGH

Allow the children to make their own play dough by mixing together:

1. 1 cup of salt
2. 2 cups of flour
3. 1 cup of water

Add food coloring to the water before mixing to create an even color throughout the play dough.

MATH

THE SNOWMAN GAME

Use a large sheet of construction paper or a file folder for the game board. Glue cut-outs of snowmen onto the board and keep hat cut-outs in an envelope attached to the outside of the game board. Children match the numbers on the hats to the number of buttons on each snowman.

SNOWFLAKES

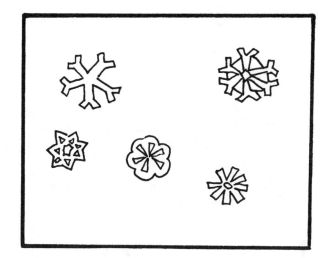

Cut out a variety of snowflakes and then trace the patterns onto a large sheet of paper. The children match the snowflake to its proper pattern on the paper.

NUMERICAL PENGUINS

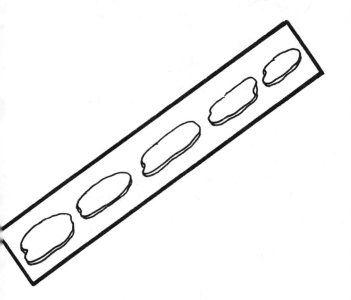

Use the penguin patterns from page 99 to make 10 penguins for this math activity. Children place them in numerical order on their ice bergs.

THE MITTEN GAME

Place brightly colored mitten cut-outs on a game board and label them with numbers from 1 to 10. Have small white circles (snowballs) available for the children to place on the mittens according to their numbers.

SOUND

Silly Snowmen

Ss

Bring in colored play dough from the science area and allow the children to make snowmen. Provide colored small candies to be used for eyes, nose, mouth and buttons. Small sticks or twigs could be used for arms.

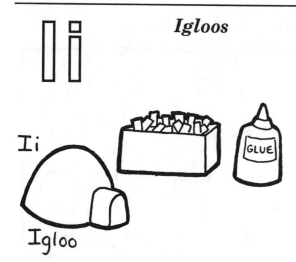

Ice Cream

 Ii

Provide cut-outs of ice cream scoops made from various colors of construction paper as well as ice cream cones cut out of brown construction paper. Children can create a giant ice cream cone by gluing pieces together. Finally, have them write alternating upper case and lower case "Ii's" on the scoops to reinforce the sound which they are learning.

Igloos

Ii

Draw an outline of an igloo on colored construction paper. Do one of these for each child. Provide small squares of white construction paper that the children can glue on to the igloo to resemble snow.

Quilts

Qq

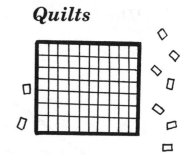

This project can be done in two different ways:

1) Mark off squares on a large sheet of white paper and allow the children to decorate them as they wish.

2) Provide squares of various wall paper patterns that the children can glue into place on the large white paper.

(If possible, bring in a real patchwork quilt for the children to examine.)

LIBRARY

The Mitten	by Alvin Tresselt
White Snow, Bright Snow	by Alvin Tresselt
The Snowy Day	by Ezra Jack Keats
Katy And The Big Snow	by Virginia Lee Buton
Winter	by Fern Hollow
In Winter	by Jane Belk Moncure

MUSIC

Over The River And Through The Woods

Frosty The Snowman

Winter Wonderland

Sleigh Ride

Jingle Bells

CLASS ACTIVITIES

SNOWCONES

Borrow a snowcone machine. Crush ice in the machine to make snow. Sprinkle syrup, jello powder or fruit juice on top. Scoop into small paper cups and let the children enjoy their unusual treat!

SLEDDING FUN

Plan a field trip. Ask parents for assistance in providing sleds. Remember to dress warmly and bring extra mittens with you!

ICE SKATING

Spend an hour or two at the ice skating rink or consider taking your class to a local community center for ice skating lessons! Always make sure there is plenty of adult supervision.

HOT CHOCOLATE

On a cold or blustery day, make hot chocolate with marshmallows for a special snack.

ANGELS IN THE SNOW

Make angels in the snow outside. Have the children lie down in the snow on their backs. Have the children flap their arms and legs back and forth as far as they can. Help the children stand up carefully and turn around to see the "angels" they have created.

BUILD A SNOWMAN

Have the whole class work together to build a snowman, complete with hat, scarf and carrot nose.

SNOW-CAPPED ALPHABET LETTERS

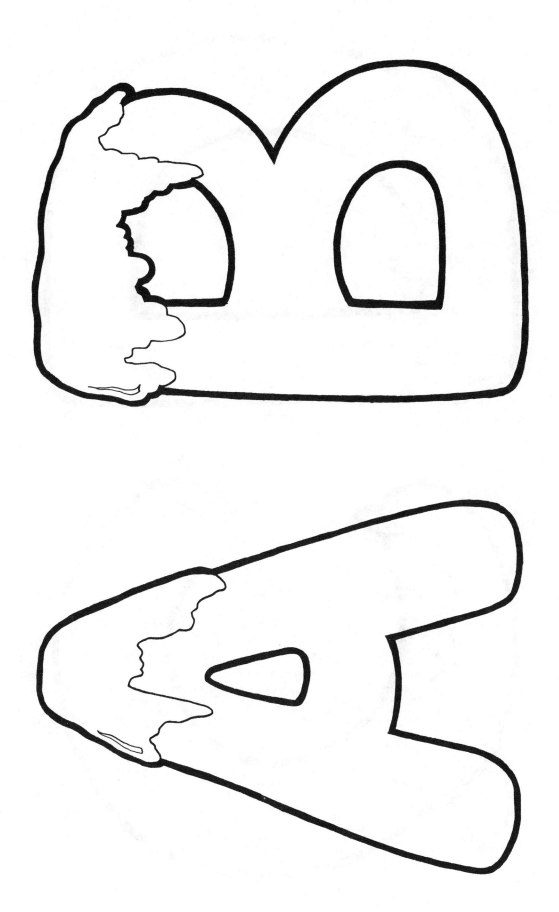

SNOW-CAPPED ALPHABET LETTERS

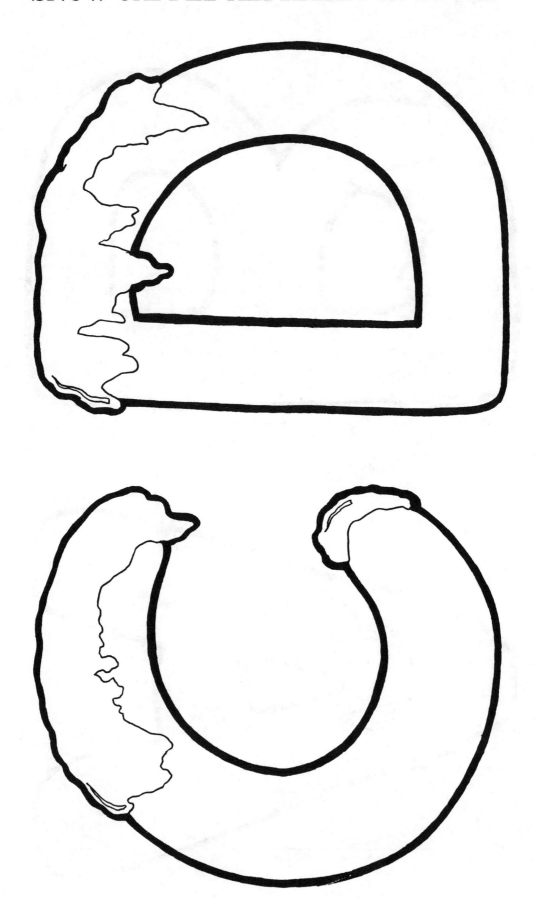

SNOW-CAPPED ALPHABET LETTERS

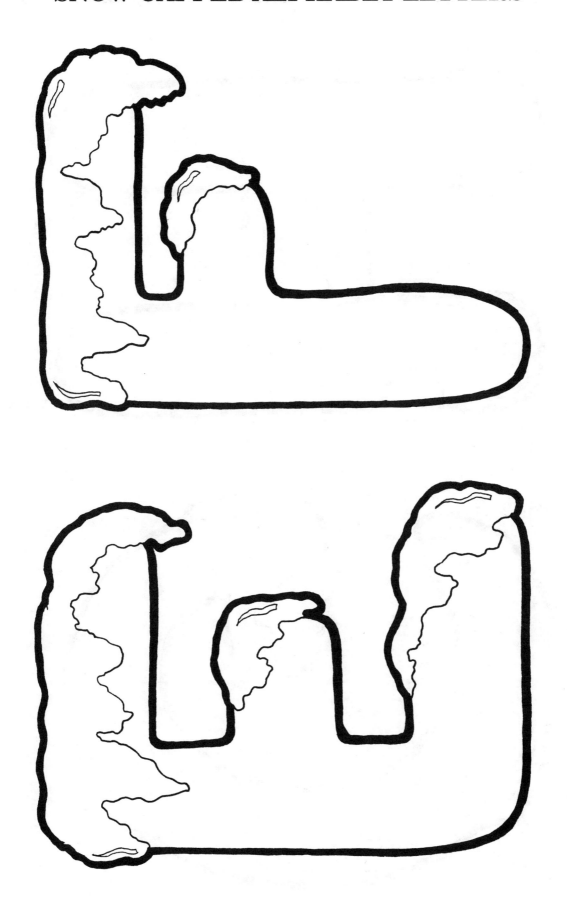

SNOW-CAPPED ALPHABET LETTERS

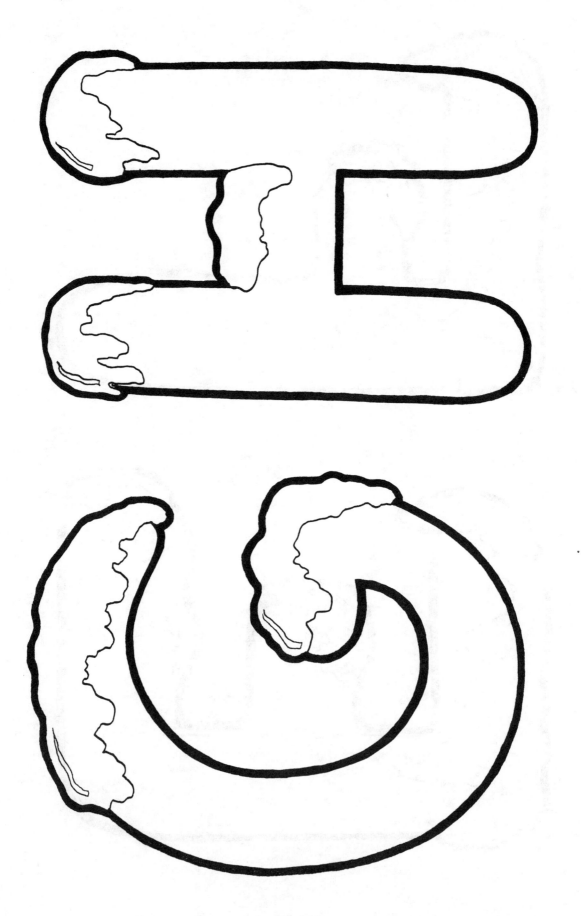

SNOW-CAPPED ALPHABET LETTERS

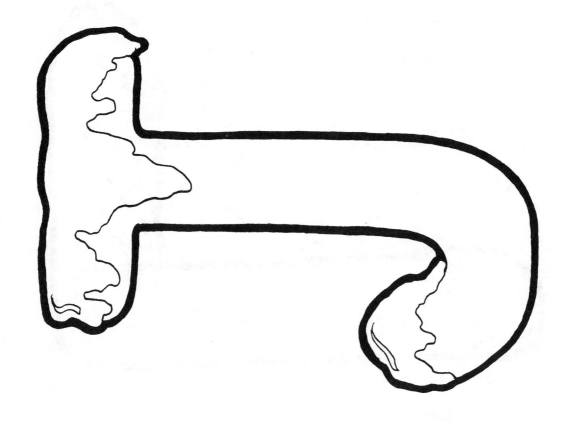

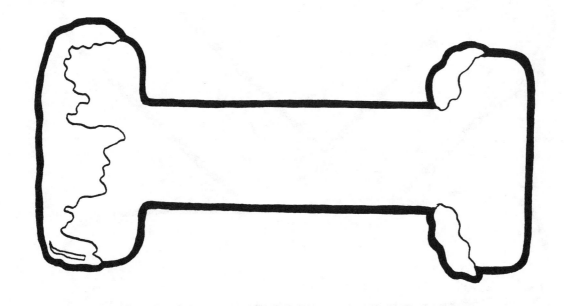

SNOW-CAPPED ALPHABET LETTERS

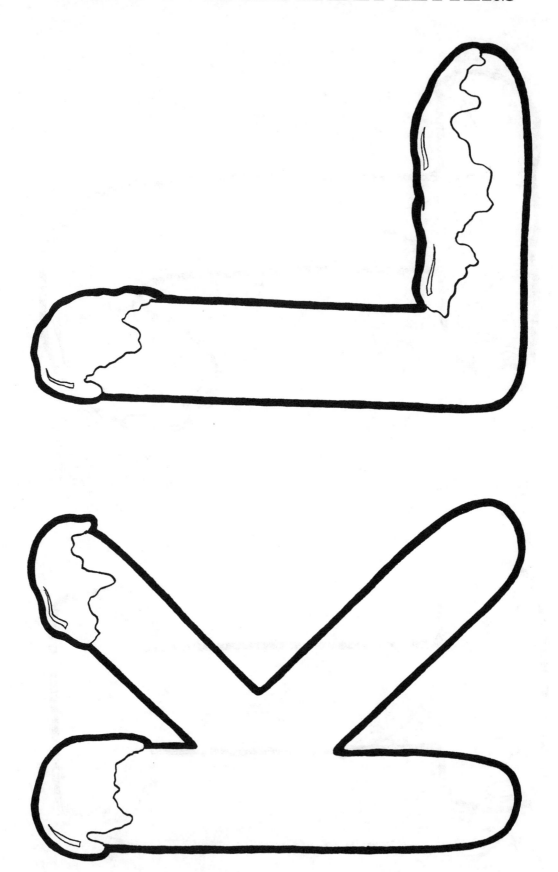

SNOW-CAPPED ALPHABET LETTERS

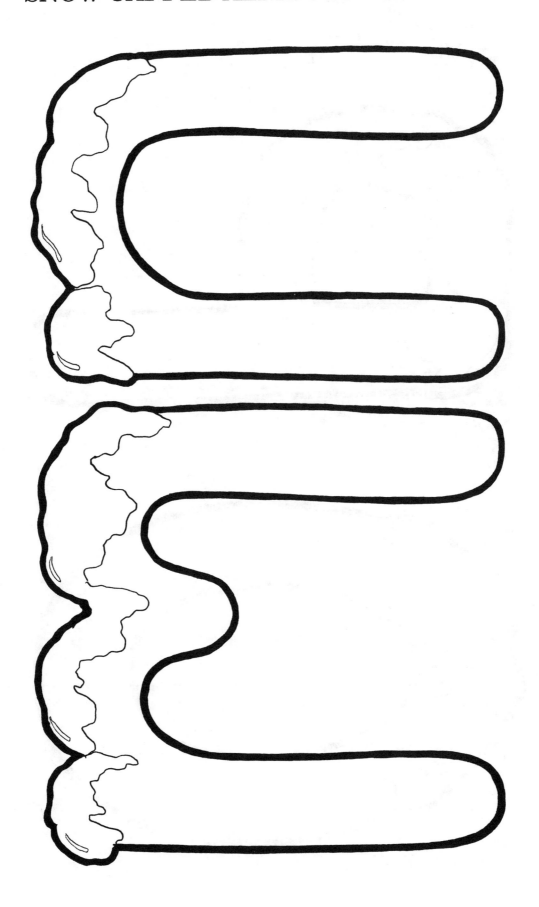

SNOW-CAPPED ALPHABET LETTERS

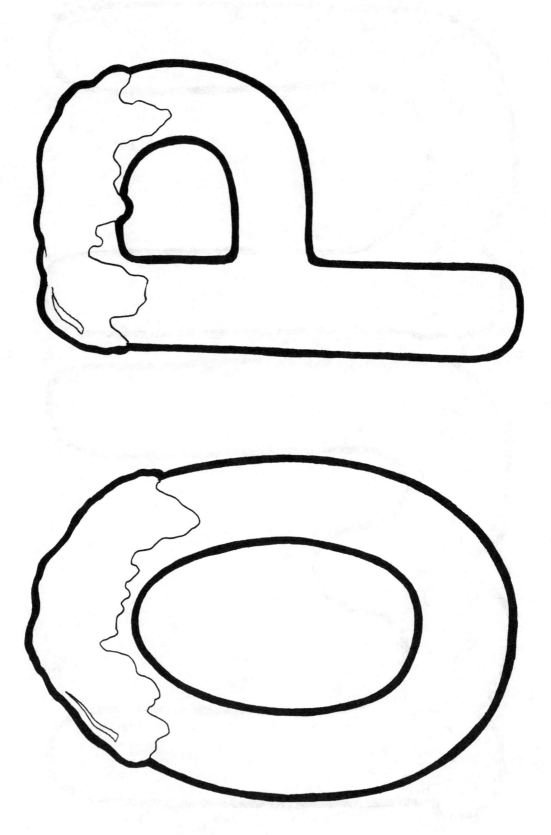

SNOW-CAPPED ALPHABET LETTERS

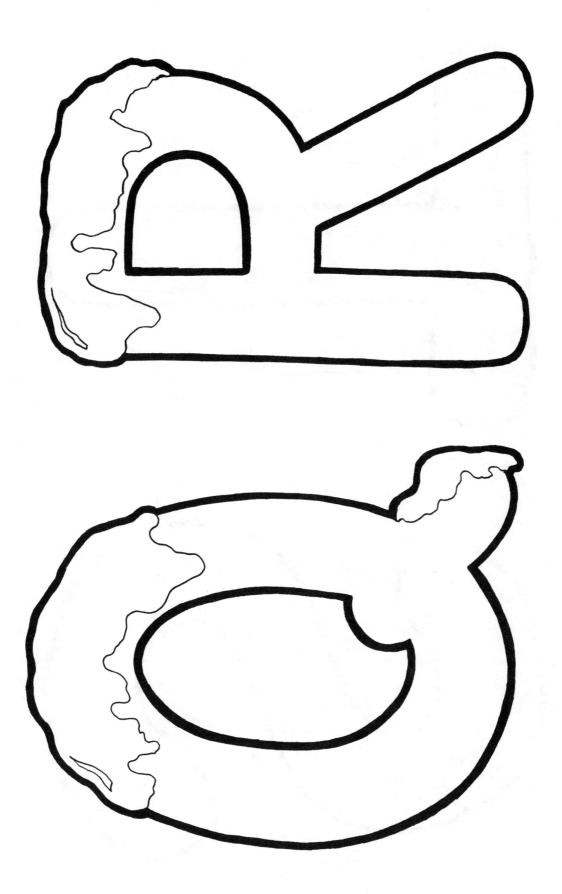

SNOW-CAPPED ALPHABET LETTERS

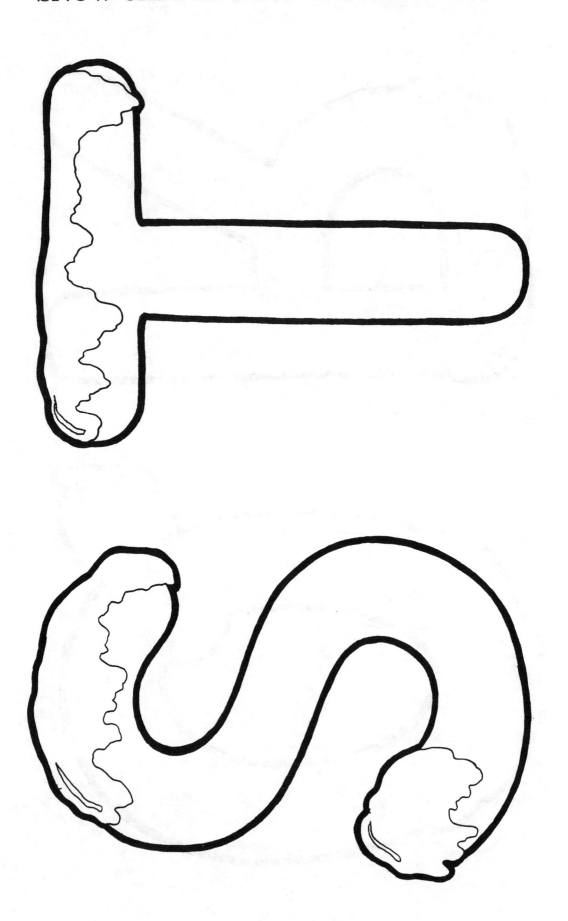

SNOW-CAPPED ALPHABET LETTERS

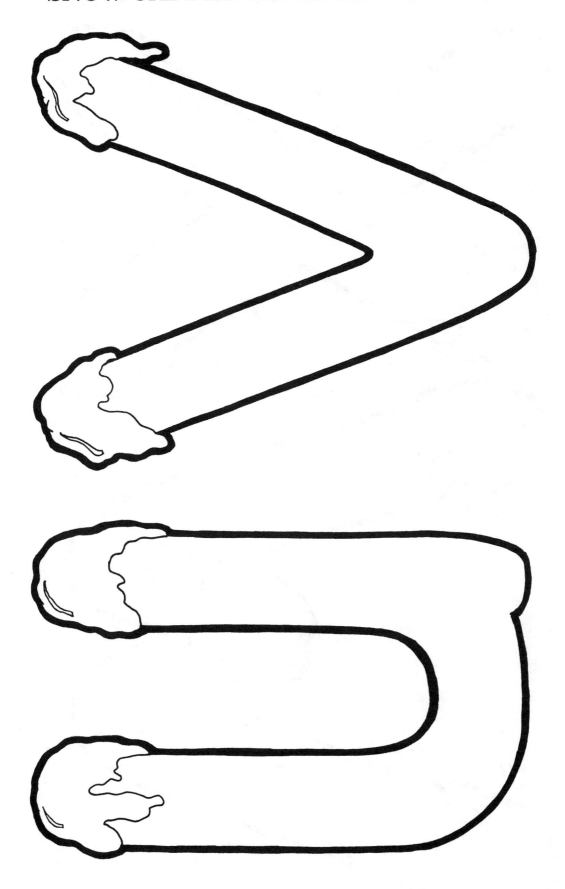

SNOW-CAPPED ALPHABET LETTERS

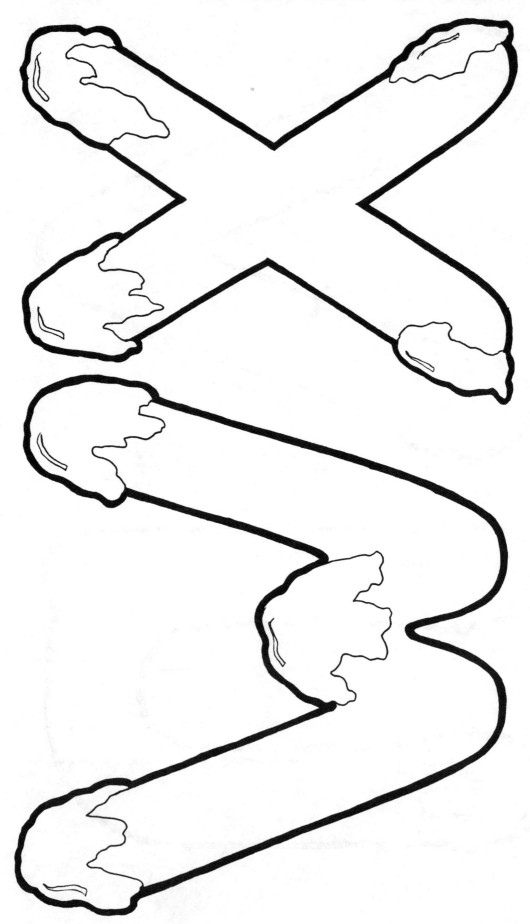

SNOW-CAPPED ALPHABET LETTERS

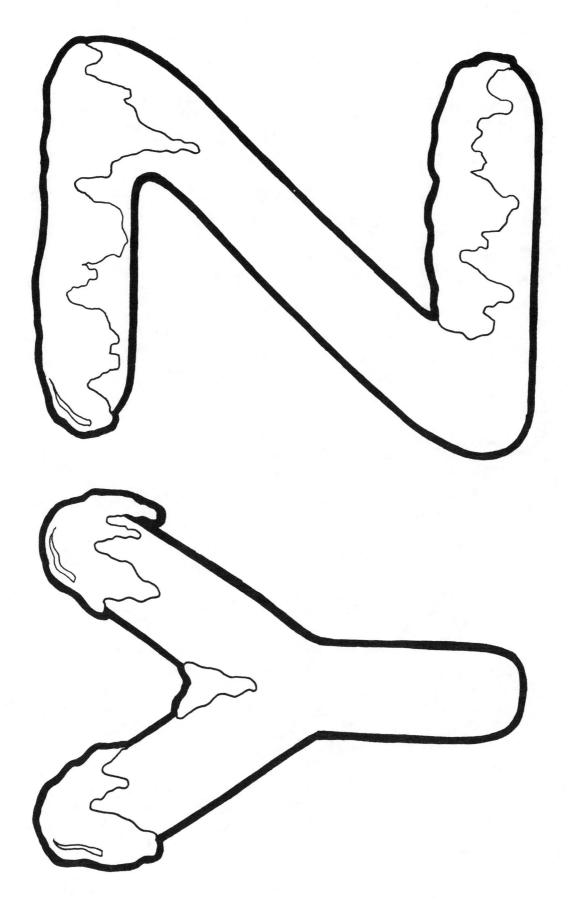

FEBRUARY

PETS

HERBIE

HERBIE

HERBIE

February

CALENDAR

Sunday	Monday	Tuesday	Wednesday	Thursday	Friday	Saturday
				1	2	3
4	5	6	7	8	9	10
11	12	13	14	15		

Make a very large fish bowl out of heavy white paper, then color or paint the water blue. Use the pattern below to make the fish to number your calendar. The fish bowl should be large enough to hold all of the fish at the beginning of the month.

FEBRUARY
BULLETIN BOARDS

PARENT BOARD

Use the kitten pattern *(on page 144)* to make a kitten to place in the bottom corner of your Parent Board. Use a real yarn or draw a ball of yarn on construction paper and string yarn all the way around the board for a border. Take pictures of your students with their pets during a special "Pet Show & Tell" to make an extra interesting Parent Board this month.

BIRTHDAY BOARD

Use large green letters for your Birthday Board heading this month. Cut out white bunnies *(pattern included on the following page)* and orange carrots. Write each child's name and birthdate on his or her Birthday Bunny.

BUNNY PATTERN
FOR BIRTHDAY BOARD

Directions are found on page 126.

WINDOW SCENE

Use colored construction paper of your choice to make an awning for your window and the "PET SHOP" letters. You could also include an "OPEN" sign and a puppy or other animals one might find in a Pet Store. This window corresponds with the song, "How Much Is That Puppy In The Window?"

CUBBY LABEL

Turtle

Plans and Patterns for Preschool

TABLE LABEL

Mouse

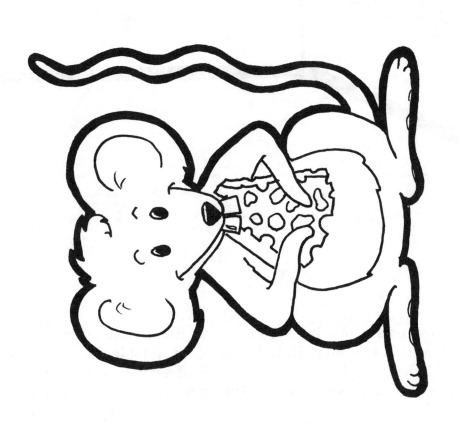

T.S. Denison & Co., Inc.

DRAMATIC PLAY

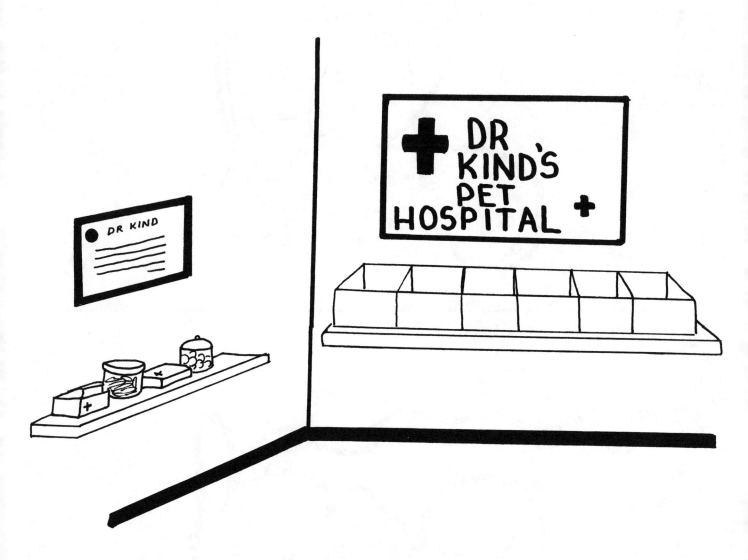

Ask your students to bring in some old stuffed animals from home that are in need of medical attention. Have boxes set up on tables or shelves to be used for cages. Medical supplies can be purchased at a department store or supplied by your local veterinarian. Make sure you have plenty of bandages.

SCIENCE

MATCH THE PETS TO THEIR HOMES

Reproduce page 132 for each student. The children can color the pictures and then draw a line from each pet to its home.

For an extra activity, ask the children to bring in the homes of their pets or pictures of them.

LUNCH TIME

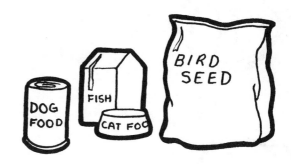

Set out some samples of various kinds of pet foods on your science table for the children to examine. Your local pet store may be willing to donate small samples.

CLASSROOM HATCHERY

Contact a local hatchery which will be able to supply you with an incubator and eggs to set up in your own classroom. This is a very educational as well as exciting experience for young children.

UNUSUAL PETS

Discuss with the children some unusual animals that people sometimes have for pets. If possible, invite some to class. If not, bring in books or a movie about unusual pets.

MATCH THE PETS
TO THEIR HOMES

Directions are found on page 131.

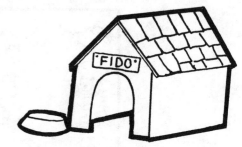

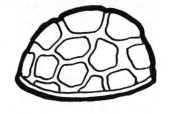

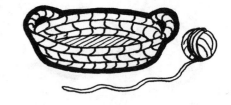

MATH

SPOT

Reproduce 10 or more pictures of "Spot" found on page 134 and write a different number on each dog's collar. Have a number of black spots available for the children to use in placing a corresponding number of spots on each dog.

BUNNIES

Reproduce and laminate 10 bunnies *(page 139)*, numbering each of them with the numbers 1 to 10. Children "feed" carrots to the bunnies according to the number each bunny is wearing.

THE DOG AND BONES

Reproduce and laminate the dog *(page 135)* and the bone patterns *(page 136)*. Children arrange the bones in order according to number and size.

GOLDFISH BOWLS

Reproduce 10 pictures of the goldfish bowl *(page 137)* with a number between 1 and 10 at the top of each bowl. Children place the appropriate number of goldfish cutouts in each bowl.

SPOT

Directions are found on page 133.

SPOT

DOG AND THE BONES

Directions are found on page 133.

DOG AND THE BONES

Directions are found on page 133.

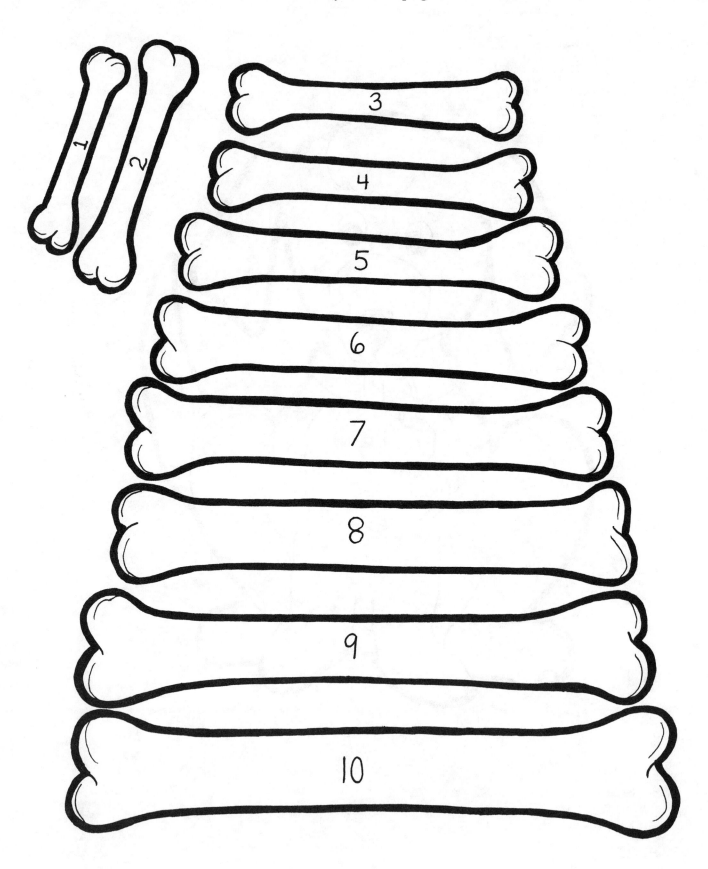

GOLDFISH BOWLS

Directions are found on page 133.

BUNNIES

Directions are found on page 133.

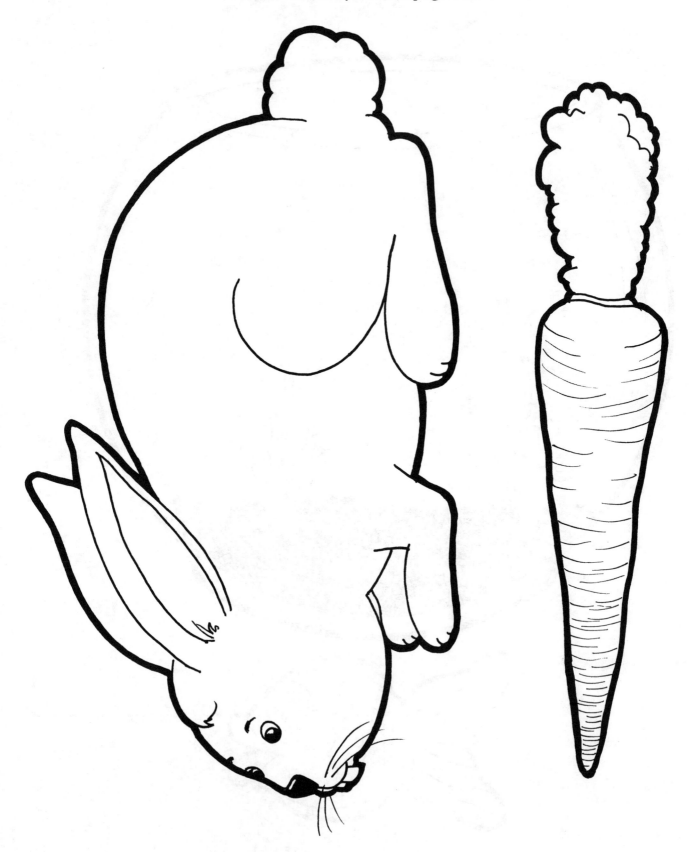

SOUND

Hh — *Hamster House*

Enlarge and reproduce this picture of a hamster in his home for the children to color. It is also fun to have a real hamster visit the classroom.

Pp — *Popcorn Pets*

Pop popcorn and allow the children to glue it onto paper in the shape of a pet.

Yy — *Yarn Pictures*

Provide large pieces of blank paper, kitten cut-outs *(pattern on page 144)* and yarn. Children can glue the kitten onto the paper and then glue on the yarn as they wish.

Yy — *Yellow*

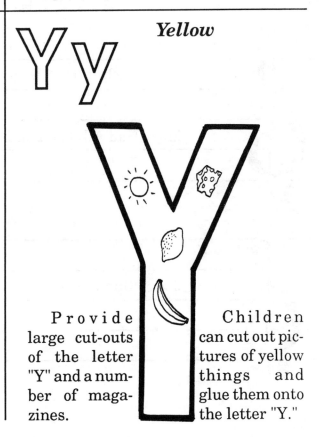

Provide large cut-outs of the letter "Y" and a number of magazines. Children can cut out pictures of yellow things and glue them onto the letter "Y."

LIBRARY

Helping Our Animal Friends	by Judith E. Rinard
Pet Shop	by Ezra Jack Keats
The Puppy Book	by Jan Pfloog
The Horse Book	by Virginia Parsons
My Goldfish	by Herbert H. Wong and Matthew F. Vessel
Clifford, The Big Red Dog	by Norman Bridwell
Curious George Walks The Pets	by Margret and H.A. Rey

MUSIC

How Much Is That Doggie In The Window

Mary Had A Little Lamb

Three Blind Mice

ART

YUMMY GOLDFISH PICTURES

Provide the children with an outline of a goldfish bowl. Have the children use crayons to draw stones and seaweed on the bottom. Next, paint over the crayon drawing with light blue water color paint. When the paint is dry, let the children glue goldfish crackers on the bowl to complete their pictures.

BIRD CAGE

Reproduce the bird cage picture on page 142 for each child. The children begin this project by coloring the bird. Finish the project by having the children glue yarn on top of the dotted lines.

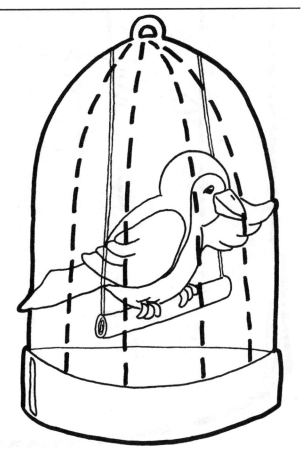

BIRD CAGE

Directions are found on page 141.

ART

PARROTS

Provide the children with large cut-outs of parrots on heavy paper or poster board. Allow the children to paint them, using bright colors of paint. Punch a hole in the top and hang them from the ceiling.

FROG PUPPETS

Reproduce the frog pattern on page 144 for each child in your class. The children can color the frog, cut it out and glue or tape it on a popsicle stick to create a frog puppet.

KITTEN AND FROG PATTERNS

Directions for the kitten are found on page 139.
Directions for the frog are found on page 143.

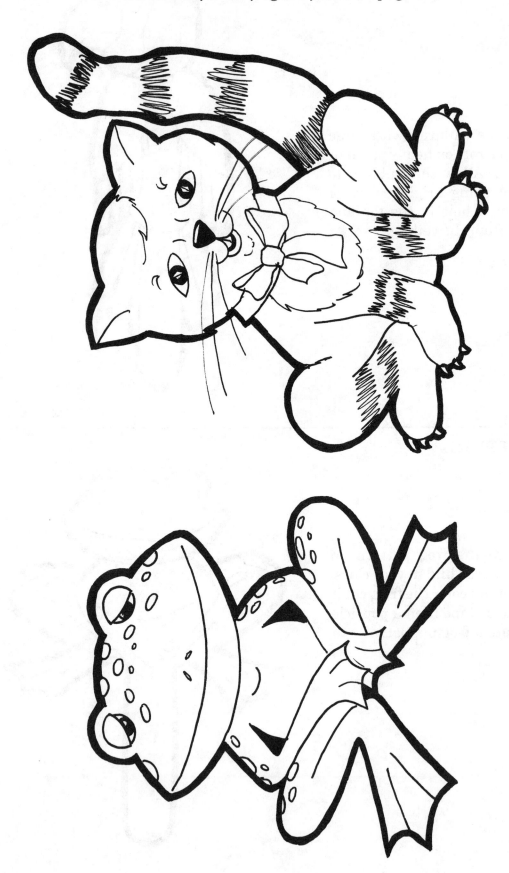

CLASS ACTIVITIES

PET STORE FIELD TRIP

Take a field trip to your local pet store. Call ahead to arrange a tour.

PET SHOW & TELL

Plan a day in which your students will be allowed to bring their pets for a very special show and tell. It works best to have the parents there during the sharing time and then ask them to bring the pets back home. If parents are working or unable to come ask the children to bring a picture of their pets to school for sharing time.

CLASSROOM PETS

Acquire a pet for the classroom. Fish, turtles, hamsters and even rabbits make wonderful classroom pets. Set up a schedule of responsibilities to ensure that each child has a chance to be included in the care of the pet.

FIELD TRIP TO A VETERINARY OFFICE

Take a field trip to a local Pet Hospital or Veterinary Office. They will often give tours and then give "care kits" to each child to use with their own pets.

VISIT AN ANIMAL SHELTER

Visit a local Animal Shelter. Explain to your students the purpose of an animal shelter before you go.

BATHING A PET

Give a pet a bath. Send a note home asking someone to donate the use of their dog for a bath given by the children at school. Make sure you use the appropriate soap and shampoo for the animal.

EXTRA FUN VALENTINE'S DAY IDEAS AND PROJECTS

VALENTINE CARD HOLDER

For this project you will need to purchase red plastic plates. Each child will need 1 full plate and ½ of another plate. Punch holes around the edge of the plates as illustrated. Have the children lace the plates together with yarn. Have the children decorate a white paper heart to glue or tape on the front of the Valentine card Holder. Finish it by punching a hole in the top and tying a bow with yarn.

CANDY BOXES

Small chipped wood boxes can be purchased inexpensively at your local craft store. Allow the children to paint the boxes with white paint. Sponge paint a pink heart on the top of the lid of the box. Fill the box with Valentine's Day candy or small cookies.

RED AND WHITE DAY

About two weeks before Valentine's day, have a "red and white" day. On that day, take pictures of each child holding a very large heart that says "I LOVE YOU!" Attach the pictures to a tagboard frame with glue or tape, and decorate the frames with Valentine's stickers. These make great gifts for parents.

VALENTINE'S DAY
PARTY TREATS

For a special treat at your Valentine's Day party, make cupcakes with a white cake mix. Just before baking add a drop or two of red food coloring to the batter. Frost the cupcakes with white icing. Add red sugar sprinkles to the top of the icing. If you wish, you could also add a drop or two of red food coloring to a carton of milk. Shake well and serve "pink" milk with the cupcakes.

DOT-TO-DOT
VALENTINE HEART

Have the children connect the dots and then decorate the heart as they wish.

MARCH

A Touch Of Spring

March

CALENDAR

Sunday	Monday	Tuesday	Wednesday	Thursday	Friday	Saturday
					1	2
3	4	5	6	7	8	9
10	11	12	13	14		

Enlarge and color the picture of the girl with an umbrella. Flowers should be falling like rain.

Cut flowers out of brightly colored construction paper, then add numbers with a black magic marker. Add stems and leaves for the "MARCH" heading.

MARCH
BULLETIN BOARDS

PARENT BOARD

Create this colorful spring Parent Board by cutting out brightly colored tulips to place at the bottom of the board and a bright yellow sun for the top corner. Cut out white paper clouds and label them with the Parent Board letters for the heading.

BIRTHDAY BOARD

Make a large kite for this Birthday Board with bows made out of construction paper. Write each child's name and birthdate on the two sides of the bow.

WINDOW SCENE

Hang brightly colored streamers from your window to make curtains and tie them back with bright red bows. Make flower pots full of tulips to line the window sill. You may also wish to make a bright yellow sun and some fluffy white clouds *(glue cotton onto white paper)*.

CUBBY LABEL
Butterfly

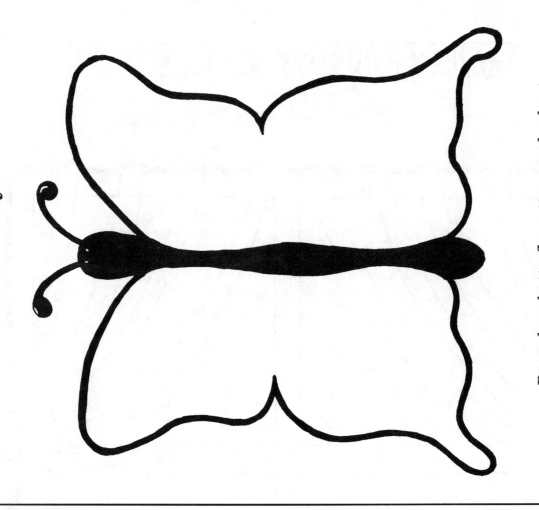

Reproduce butterfly pattern and color to make labels for the children's cubbies. You may also wish to use the pattern to cut butterflies out of brightly colored construction paper.

Plans and Patterns for Preschool

TABLE LABEL
Caterpillar

Use the pattern below to cut out brightly colored circles from construction paper. Use a black marker to write each letter of the student's name on a separate circle. Overlap circles to make a caterpillar and tape together from the back. Add an extra circle in the front for the face and antennae.

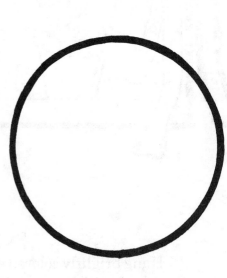

T.S. Denison & Co., Inc.

DRAMATIC PLAY

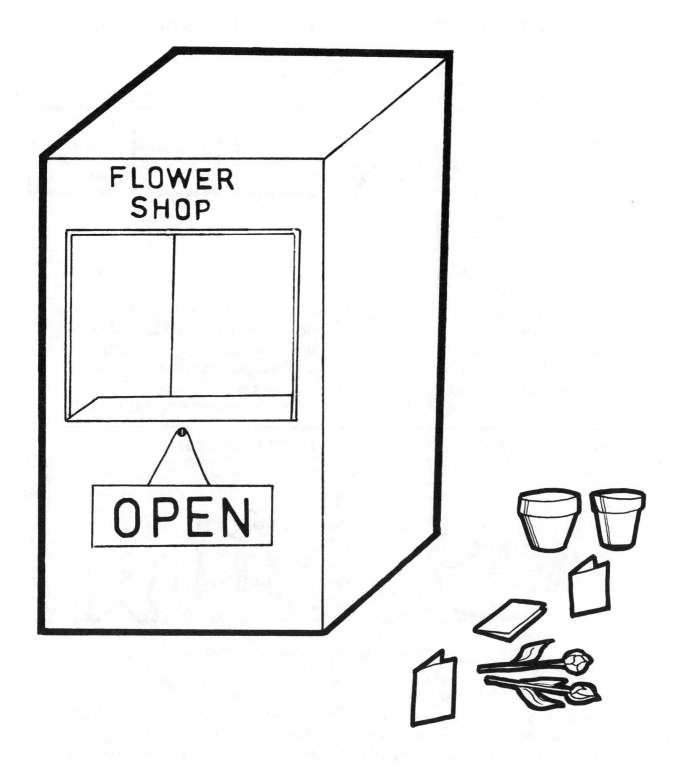

Use a large cardboard appliance box or a puppet theater to create a Flower Shop in your classroom. Include artificial flowers, flowerpots with styrofoam in them, greeting cards, tissue paper, flower boxes, a cash register and play money.

SCIENCE

TORNADO IN A BOTTLE

Fill a clear 2 liter soft drink bottle 2/3 full of water. Add 5 or 6 drops of blue food coloring and shake well. Next add 1/3 cup of vegetable oil and let it settle on top of the water. Make sure the bottle lid is screwed on tightly. Hold the bottom of the bottle in one hand and rotate the top of the bottle in a quick circular motion with the other hand. Watch a tornado appear.

THREE STAGES OF A LEAF

Reproduce a copy for each child in the class of the leaf sequencing cards, found on page 163. The students color the pictures, cut them out and then arrange the pictures in their proper sequence.

Discuss the stages of a leaf with the class before doing this project.

GRASS GARDEN

In shallow containers, such as margarine tugs, plant grass seeds which can be purchased at your local nursery. Make sure you keep them watered and give them plenty of light. Grass seeds are inexpensive so each student can plant their own grass garden.

FLYING FRIENDS

With the help of library books, films or real samples if possible, compare the similarities and differences of moths and butterflies. Many preschool age children have only heard of butterflies and may not be familiar with a moth.

LEAF SEQUENCING CARDS

Directions are found on page 162.

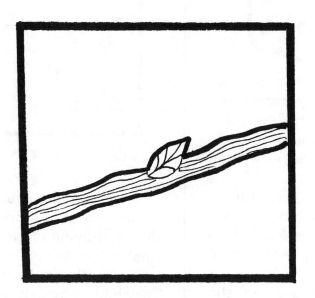

MATH

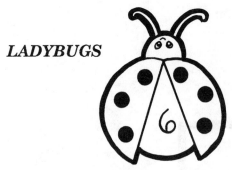

LADYBUGS

Make 10 ladybugs out of red construction paper. Add eyes and number with black marker. Have black circles available for the children to add the number of circles as written on each ladybug.

Another suggestion would be to attach the wings with brads so that the wings could move back and forth to cover the number on the ladybug. The spots should already be on the ladybug. The students count the spots and then move the wings back to see if they counted correctly.

THE KITE GAME

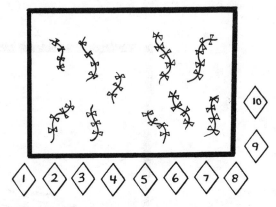

In a file folder or on a large piece of paper, draw 10 kite tails, each of the tails having 1 to 10 bows. Cut out small kites from construction paper, labeled with numbers from 1 to 10. The children match the kites to the tails with the corresponding number of bows.

FLOWER PATTERNS

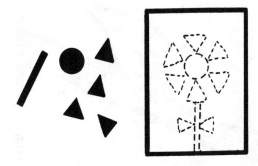

Reproduce for each child in the class a copy of the flower pattern found on page 165. Have shapes cut out of construction paper for the children to glue on to the appropriate places. You can also make and laminate just one flower pattern and let the children use it as a puzzle and experiment with placing different colored shapes on the flower.

NUMERICAL ORDER

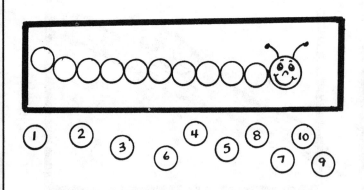

On a long strip of paper, make a picture like the one above. Use the circle patterns for the "Table Label," found on page 160. The children arrange the circles in numerical order from 1 to 10.

FLOWER PATTERN

Directions are found on page 164.

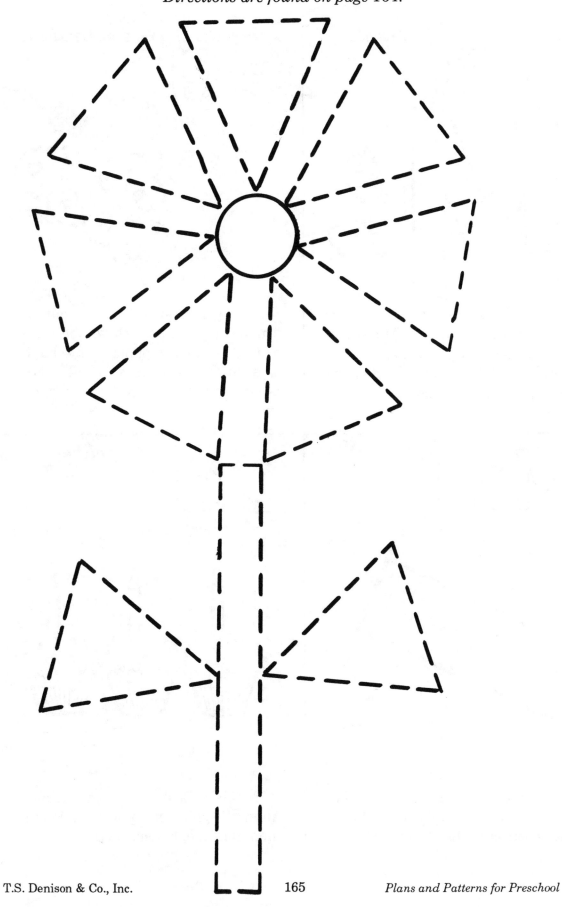

SOUND

M&Ms

Cut "M" shapes out of heavy paper or poster board. Allow the children to glue on M&M's, making sure the "m" side is on top. Be sure there are extra candies left for sampling!

Green Grapes

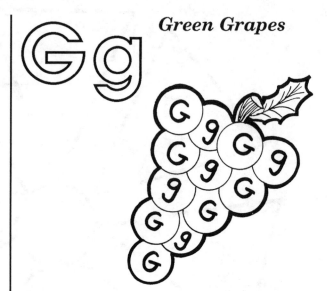

Cut green grape circles out of construction paper. Have the children glue them on paper in the shape of a cluster of grapes. Then write upper and lower case Gg's on each circle.

March

Enlarge a copy of this picture for each child to color. Have the children "march" around the classroom.

Cupcakes

Make cupcakes for snacktime. Allow the children to put candles in them for an extra special treat.

ART

WIND SOCK

1. Have the children draw brightly colored pictures on 12" x 18" pieces of construction paper.
2. Roll the paper into a tube and tape together.
3. Staple yarn to the top to make a hanger.
4. On the inside of the bottom, tape brightly colored streamers to complete the wind sock.

KITES

Give each child a large piece of heavy paper in the shape of a kite. Have the children decorate their kites with crayons, markers, paints and bits of ribbon. Add yarn or string for the kite tails and tape on ribbons.

ART

LADY BUGS

Using the patterns included on pages 169 & 170, cut two large circles out of construction paper; one black and one red. Cut the red circle in half and add black paper spots to make the ladybug's wings. Glue the wings onto the black circle body. Then add a smaller circle, in black, for the head. Finally, add the eyes and antennae. Hang the ladybugs from the ceiling.

BUMBLE BEE

 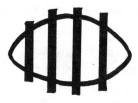 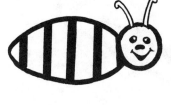 

The patterns for the bumble bee are found on page 171. Cut the body and the head for each bee out of yellow construction paper. Cut stripes, legs, and antennae out of black construction paper. Glue black stripes onto the body of the bee, then trim them next to the yellow paper. Glue on the head and draw a face. Add the antennae and legs. Cut wings out of wax paper and glue onto the body to complete the bumble bee. These look cute hanging from the ceiling along with the ladybugs.

LADYBUG PATTERNS

Directions found on page 168.

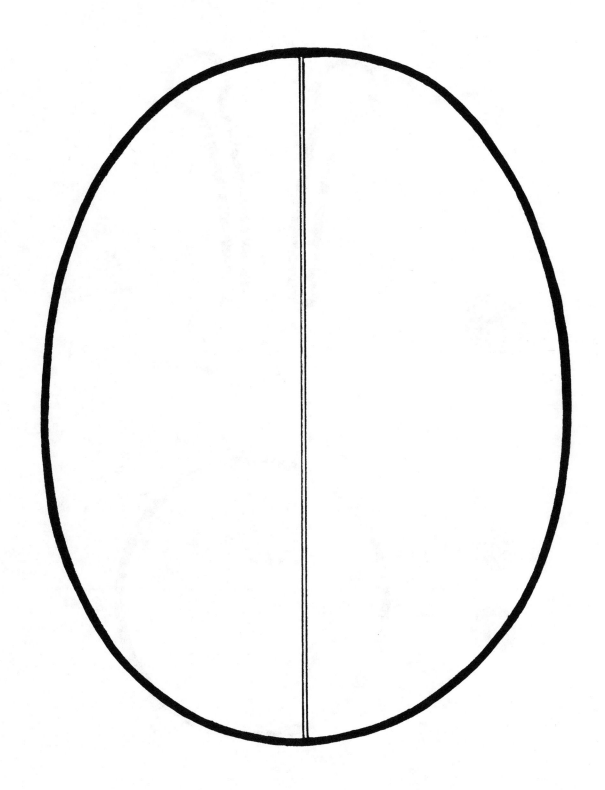

LADYBUG PATTERNS

Directions found on page 168.

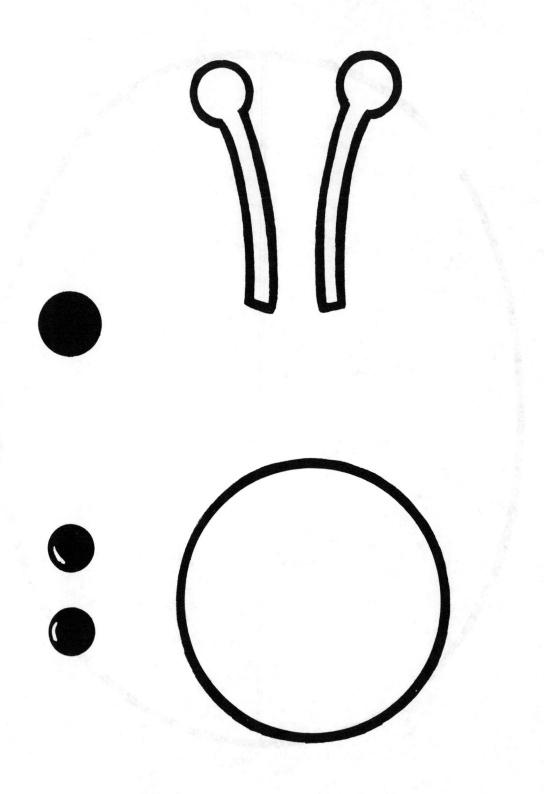

BUMBLE BEE PATTERNS

Directions found on page 168.

LIBRARY

Spring	by Fern Hollow
Rain	by Peter Spier
Taste The Raindrop	by Anna Grossnickle Hines
Eric Plants A Garden	by Jean Hudlow
The Butterfly	by Paula Z. Hogan
Once We Went On A Picnic	by Aileen Fisher
Winnie The Pooh And The Blustery Day	by A.A. Milne

MUSIC

Let's Go Fly A Kite *(from The Mary Poppins Musical)*

Here We Go Round The Mulberry Bush

Ring Around The Rosey

CLASS ACTIVITIES

FLY A KITE

Buy or make kites to fly outdoors on a windy day!

YOUR LOCAL FLOWER SHOP

Take a field trip to a local flower shop or have a florist come and visit your classroom. Purchase an arrangement to brighten your classroom.

A BUTTERFLY HUNT

Butterfly nets can be purchased inexpensively at most large toy stores. Take them to a park and see if you can catch any butterflies without hurting them. Then let them go!

AN OUTDOOR GARDEN

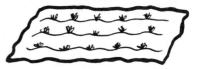

Plant a garden outdoors. Children love to watch things grow! Let them do the planting, the weeding, and the harvesting.

Beans, radishes, carrots and potatoes are some of the most successful vegetables to grow.

You can also plant flowers.

BIRD NEST SNACKS

Make Birds Nests for a special snack!

1. Bring to a boil 1/2 cup butter, 1 cup sugar and 1 cup light corn syrup.

2. Remove from heat and add 1 cup of peanut butter and 6 cups of Cheerio cereal.

3. Shape into birds nests.

4. Add M&Ms or jelly beans for eggs.

PICNIC LUNCH

Have your students prepare a picnic lunch of peanut butter and jelly sandwiches, chips, carrots, apples, brownies, and juice. Take your lunch to the park if possible. If not, eat your picnic lunch outside at your center. If you live in a colder climate, spread out a blanket on your classroom floor and have an indoor picnic.

EXTRA FUN EASTER IDEAS AND PROJECTS

EASTER BASKET
WALL DISPLAY

Enlarge this pattern to make a brown Easter Basket to display on your classroom wall. Give the children white paper eggs and have them paint the eggs with water colors. Tape the eggs into the basket to make an attractive display.

RABBIT EAR HEADBANDS

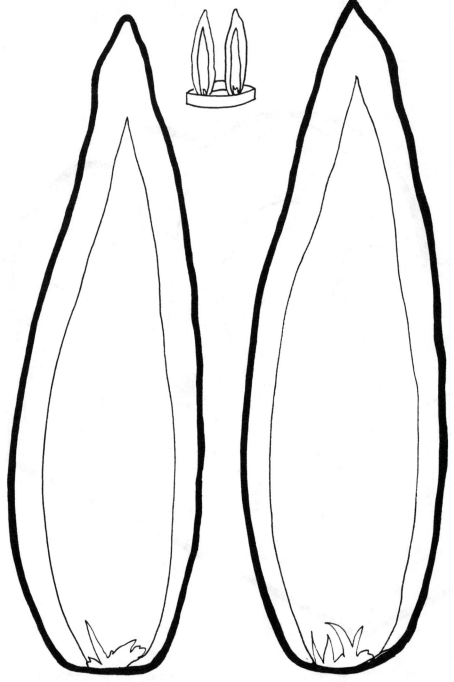

Make rabbit ear headbands for your students by cutting a 1 1/2" inch wide strip of white heavy paper. Cut the strip long enough to fit a child's head. Fit the strips to each child's head and then fasten with tape. Cut two rabbit ears out of the same paper and have the children color the insides of the ears pink. Attach the ears to the headbands with tape and have a "bunny parade" around the center.

EASTER BASKETS

Make Easter baskets for your children by attaching pipe cleaners to green plastic strawberry baskets. Add Easter grass and fill with jelly beans, small boxes of raisins, Easter eggs that you may have dyed at school or any other small treats.

HOT CROSS BUNS

Many early childhood programs do not discuss the real meaning of Easter with the students. If you are teaching in a Christian program this is an activity that you will truly enjoy.

Talk about Easter as the time when Jesus died on the cross and rose again. Make Hot Cross Buns, using a ready-to-bake package of biscuits. While the biscuits are still warm, make a cross on them with white icing.

EASTER EGG COOKIES

Use an egg-shaped cookie cutter and make Easter Egg cookies out of already prepared sugar cookie dough. Add food coloring to egg yolks. Children can use this "paint" to decorate the cookies using new paintbrushes. It will dry to a glossy finish and is completely edible.

SPRINGTIME CHICKS

Use the patterns provided above to make springtime chicks. Discuss the circle and triangle shapes you are using as you glue the pieces onto a green felt background. You will need: green, orange, and yellow felt for this project, as well as moving eyes.

APRIL

&

HEALTH

FITNESS

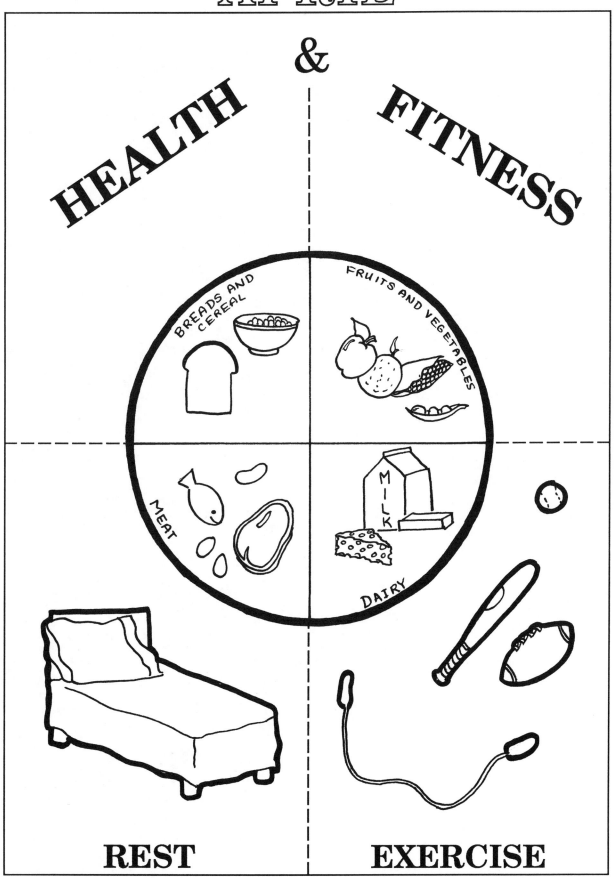

REST

EXERCISE

April

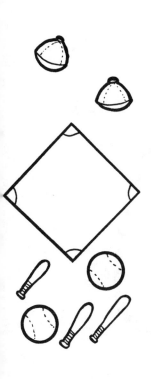

Sunday	Monday	Tuesday	Wednesday	Thursday	Friday	Saturday
					1	2
3	4	5	6	7	8	9
10	11	12				

Use a large piece of green poster board or heavy paper to make a baseball diamond. Make the bases on the corners tan or white. Reproduce the patterns included for the baseball hats (APRIL), baseballs and bats.

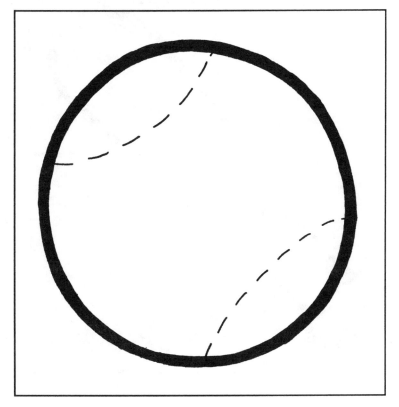

CALENDAR PATTERNS

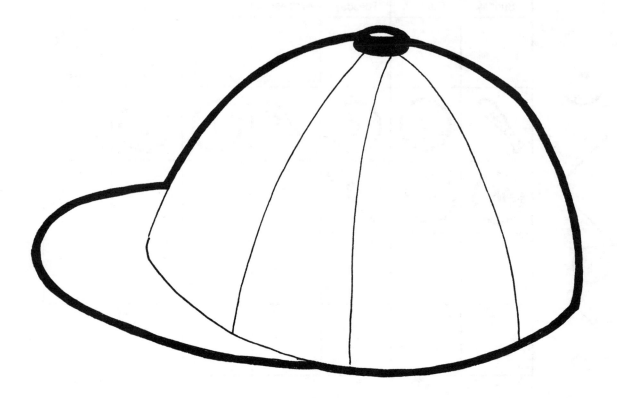

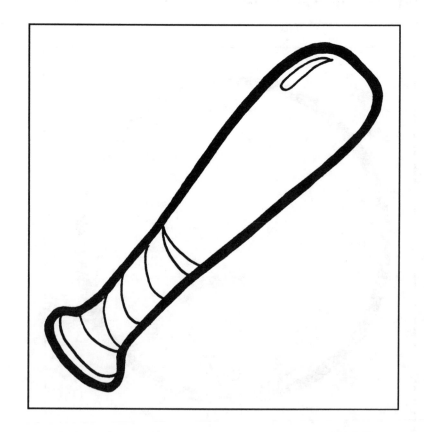

APRIL
BULLETIN BOARDS

PARENT BOARD

Make waves on the bottom of your Parent Board with light blue paper. Create the Parent Board heading by cutting out and coloring rings that look like life preservers and writing Parent Board letters inside them.

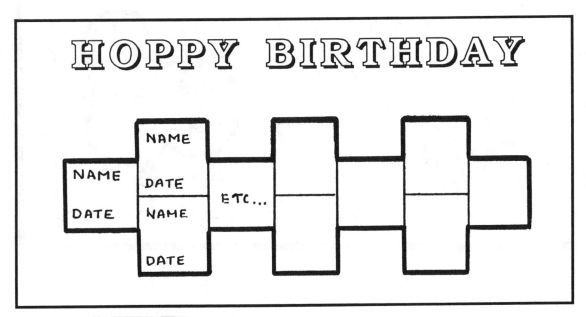

BIRTHDAY BOARD

Draw a large hopscotch game on this month's Birthday Board. Write each student's name and birthdate in a hopscotch square. Lable the board "HOPPY BIRTHDAY!"

WINDOW SCENE

Enlarge these patterns and color them with bright colors. Use them as a discussion starter concerning the four basic food groups. If possible, place your science center near this window.

CUBBY LABEL

Workout Weight

Make workout weights for cubby labels. Allow your students to choose what color they want their own label to be.

Plans and Patterns for Preschool

TABLE LABEL

Pillow Case

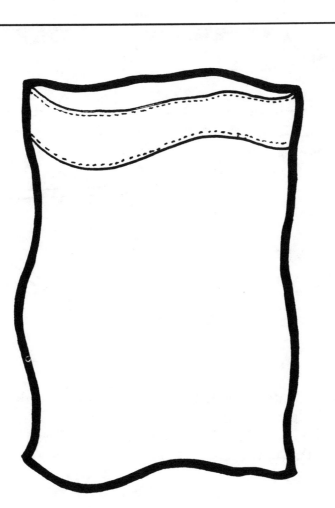

Make pillow cases for table labels as a reminder to your students that rest is an important part of good health.

T.S. Denison & Co., Inc.

DRAMATIC PLAY

FITNESS
CENTER

Create a Fitness Center in your Dramatic Play area in which your students can "work out." Include tumbling mats, ankel or wrist weights, towels, water and paper cups, and a tape recorder with a "work out" tape. Be sure to supervise and to discuss safety in this play area.

SCIENCE

A FOOD GROUP A WEEK

THE DAIRY GROUP

Concentrate on the Dairy Group during the first week of April.

• Discuss the differences between skim, 1%, 2%, and whole milk. Allow the children to sample each type.
• Bring in a variety of cheese types and have a cheese sampling party.
• Make butter by shaking whipping cream in a small glass jar. Add yellow food coloring if desired.
• Sample various flavors of ice cream and yogurt.

THE BREAD AND CEREAL GROUP

Concentrate on the Bread and Cereal Group during the second week of April.

• Bake your own bread. Discuss and sample the various kinds of breads that are available.
• Have children bring in empty cereal boxes from home. Compare nutritional values by examining the ingredients in the boxes.
• Make a pasta collage.

THE MEAT GROUP

Concentrate on the Meat Group during the third week of April.

• Spend a large amount of time in the meat department of a grocery store discussing the various kinds of meats that are available.
• High-protein foods are also in the Meat Group. Make your own peanut butter by grinding peanuts in a blender or food processor.

THE FRUIT AND VEGETABLE GROUP

Concentrate on the Fruit and Vegetable Group during the fourth week of April.

• Examine various kinds of fruits and vegetables in the various states, such as raw, cooked, juiced, canned, or jellied.
• Ask parents to get involved and provide your class with different fruit and/or vegetable salads to sample.

MATH

1,2,3

1, 2, 3...

Children understand the concept of numbers and counting much better when they have something in front of them to count, rather than rote memorization of numbers.

Get the whole class involved in counting during the "King of Fitness" *(page 194)* contest. Make this contest fun and not a threatening experience.

THE SWIMMING RACE

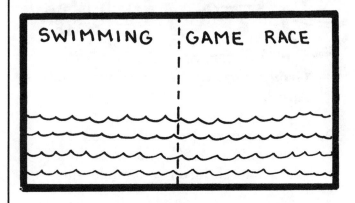

Reproduce the swimmer pattern, found on page 193, 10 times. Number each of the 10 swimmers from 1 to 10. Make a large game board, such as the one illustrated above. Children arrange the swimmers in numerical order.

WHERE IS MY PULSE?

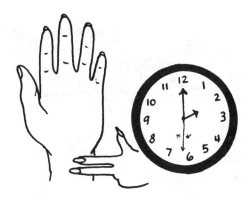

Teach your students how to take their pulse rate. Explain how exercising will cause changes in your pulse rate. Then help the children find their pulses and count with them to see what their heart rate is.

RECORD YOUR WEIGHT

Make a chart to record your students' weights. Once again, this is not meant to cause underweight or overweight children to feel uncomfortable. It is meant to be a fun experience whereby children can learn more about themselves.

SWIMMER PATTERN

Directions are found on page 192.

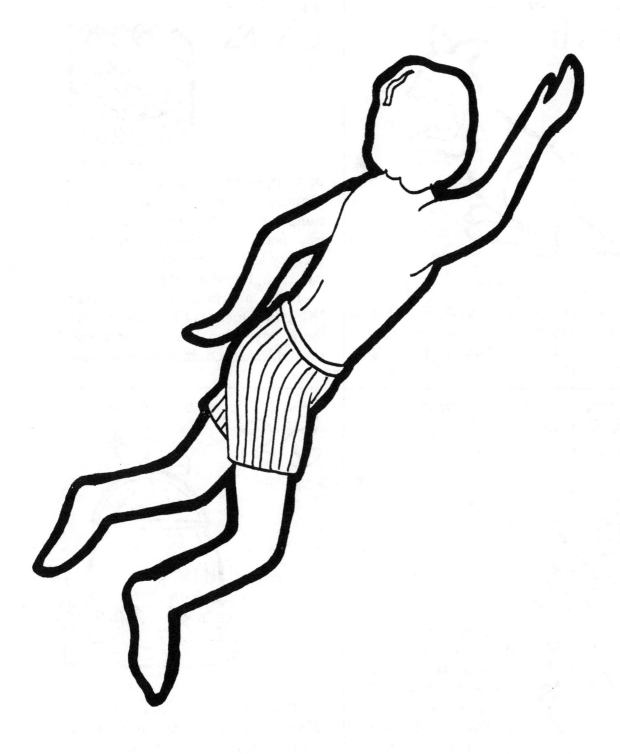

SOUND

Kk
Katy

Read H.A. Rey's book, *Katy No-Pocket,* about a kangaroo who has no pocket and therefore no place to carry her young.

Kk
King Of Fitness

Have a "King of Fitness" contest in your class. Keep records of the number of times each student can jump rope, do sit-ups, push-ups, or how fast each child can run. This activity ties in with the math activity, 1,2,3, found on page 192.

Have a crown ready for your "King (or Queen) of Fitness to wear for a day. Also have other prizes available so each child can win something.

Ss
Sammy

Teach your students the words and actions from Hap Palmer's "Sammy." They will be able to fly like a bird, swim like a fish, crawl like a bug, and hop like a bunny to the store.

Ss
Stone Soup

Read the book, *Stone Soup,* by Marcia Brown. Then make stone soup for lunch one day. Make sure the stone is scrubbed well and boiled clean.

LIBRARY

The Berenstain Bears Go To The Doctor	by Stan and Jan Berenstain
The Berenstain Bears Visit The Dentist	by Stan and Jan Berenstain
Some Busy Hospital	by Seymour Reit
Nicky Goes To The Doctor	by Richard Scarry
Sports	by Wonder Starters, A Division of Grosset & Dunlap, Inc.

MUSIC

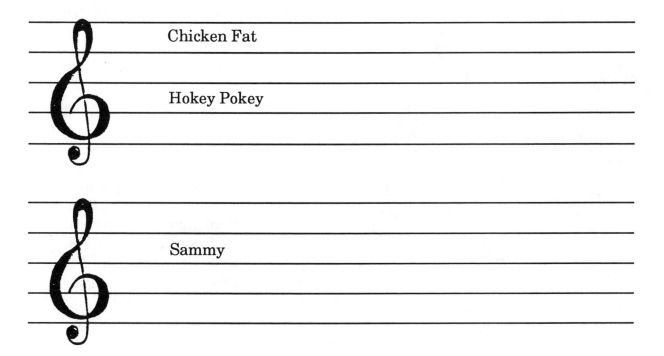

Chicken Fat

Hokey Pokey

Sammy

ART

A PAPER PLATE MEAL

Give each student a paper plate and cut-outs of food. Ask the children to create a meal which includes an item from each of the four food groups.

A HEALTH MOBILE

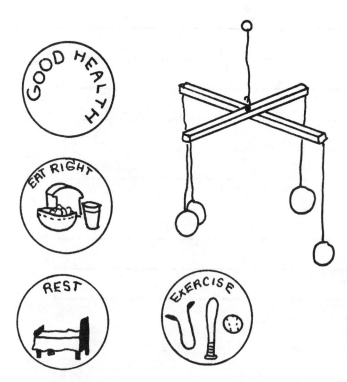

Create a health mobile. Reproduce the patterns at the left for each child. Have the children color the pictures, cut them out, and punch a hole in the top of each one. String yarn through the holes and glue or tie each string to the end of a popsicle stick. Glue the sticks together in the shape of an "X" and tie another piece of string around the center. Tie the yarn into a loop at the top and hang from the ceiling.

ART

HAPPY TOOTH

Supply each student with a copy of a large Happy Tooth *(pattern found on page 198)*. Have the children cut pictures out of magazines of foods and other things that are good for teeth, such as apples or toothpaste. Have each child glue their pictures onto their large Happy Tooth. Display all the Happy Teeth in the classroom.

You could also make a Sad Tooth and glue on pictures of foods that are not good for your teeth.

SWEATBANDS

Make sweatbands for your exercise time! Stretch headbands can be purchased inexpensively at a local department store. You will also need to purchase fabric paints, available at most craft stores. Allow the children to decorate their own sweatbands with their name or small pictures.

HAPPY TOOTH PATTERN

Directions are found on page 197.

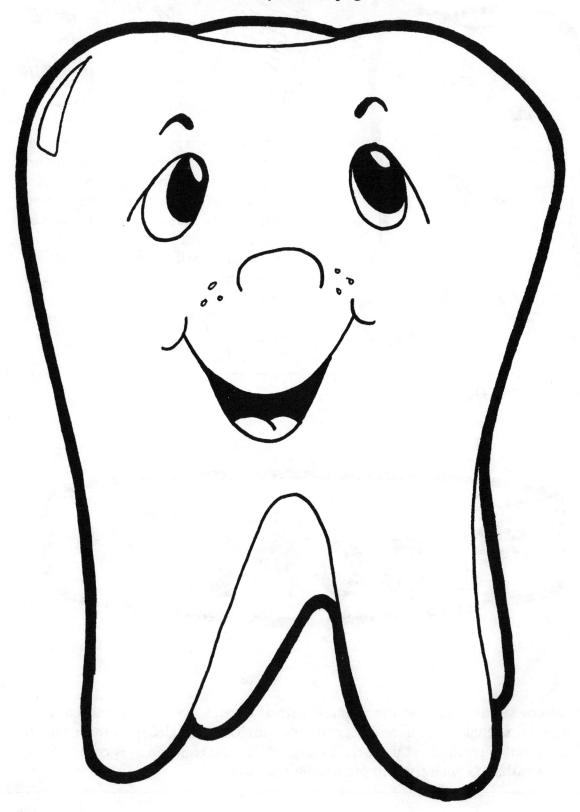

CLASS ACTIVITIES

EXERCISE EVERY DAY

Exercise together daily! There are many children's exercise records and cassette tapes available if you wish, or exercise to a video!

MAKE A PIZZA FOR LUNCH

Make a pizza for lunch using foods from all of the four food groups. The pizza crust is a member of the Bread & Cereal Group. The tomato paste is from the Fruit and Vegetable Group. Use pepperoni or hamburger from the Meat Group and cheese from the Dairy Group.

GROCERY STORE

Take a field trip to a local grocery store. Pay particularly close attention to foods which you have discussed with your class. While you are there, purchase ingredients for making the Pizza-Making Activity.

HOPSCOTCH

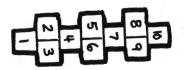

Draw a hopscotch game on the sidewalk or pavement to be used during playground time. You can also use masking tape to make a hopscotch indoors.

FIELD TRIPS TO:

1. An Optomitrist
2. A Dental Office
3. A Hospital
4. A Fitness Center

If it is not possible to visit all these places, invite professionals from these places to come and visit your classroom.

BABY PICTURES

As you are discussing ways to increase your chances of growing up healthy, it would be fun to see how much the children have already grown in their three or four years. Ask the children to bring in baby pictures of themselves to compare to how they look now!

MAY

Life On The Farm

May

CALENDAR

Sunday	Monday	Tuesday	Wednesday	Thursday	Friday	Saturday
				1	2	3
4	5	6	7	8	9	10
11	12	13	14			

Make a large apple tree out of brown and green paper. Then reproduce and color the pattern below to make the apples. Label each apple with a number for each day of May. Make three extra apples for the "MAY" heading.

MAY
BULLETIN BOARDS

PARENT BOARD

Enlarge the scarecrow pattern found on page 218. Make it large enough to be taller than the corn you will need to cut out of construction paper. Color the scarecrow and have it guard the field of corn during the month of May.

BIRTHDAY BOARD

Enlarge the mother duck pattern featured in the above illustration. Reproduce enough baby ducks *(pattern found on the following page)* so that each child will have one to label his or her name and birthdate. You could also have the mother duck standing in the pond made out of blue construction paper, leading her babies to the pond for their first swimming experience.

BABY DUCK PATTERN

Directions are found on page 204.

WINDOW SCENE

Use paint or paper to make the fence and apple trees. It is also fun to make barns with silos and pigs. *(Patterns included on page 207.)* The barns and pigs can be scattered behind the fence and in the background.

PIG PATTERN

Reproduce this pattern on pink construction paper in two pieces; one for the head and one for the nose. Glue a cotton ball on the back of the nose and then glue it on the head to complete the pig. This will give the nose a three-dimensional look.

CUBBY LABEL
Sheep

TABLE LABEL
Pig

Plans and Patterns for Preschool

T.S. Denison & Co., Inc.

DRAMATIC PLAY

Use a large cardboard appliance box or a puppet theatre to create a produce stand. Include real or plastic fruits and vegetables, paper grocery sacks and play money.

SCIENCE

FARM AND ZOO ANIMALS

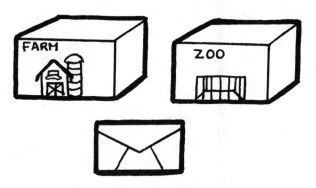

For the science center you will need two boxes and an envelope of animal pictures. Label one box with a picture of a farm animal and the other box with a picture of a zoo animal. Children sort the animals according to where they live and put them in the appropriately labeled box.

SEQUENCING CARDS
Enlarge and make into cards.

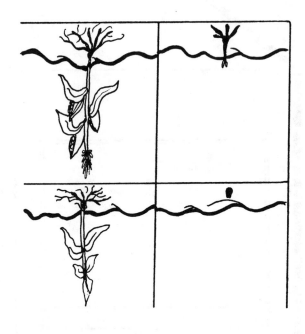

FLOWERS AND WEEDS

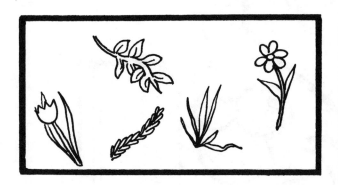

Draw pictures of flowers and weeds on a sheet of paper or cut them out of a seed catalog and glue on paper. Reproduce a copy for each child. Have the children put an "X" on each weed and circle each flower.

SAMPLES OF FOOD GROWN ON A FARM

Put samples of various kinds of farm products on the science table for the children to examine and taste. Examples would include various colors of apples, brown and white eggs and different types of cheese.

MATH

THE WATERMELON GAME

Cut large wedge-shaped pieces of watermelon out of red construction paper. Color a green rim around each curved edge. Label each piece with a number between 1 and 10. Have the children place the appropriate number of watermelon seeds on each piece of watermelon.

THE WORM PUZZLE

Make a large apple gameboard from heavy red paper. Make the worm out of green construction paper, labeling it as shown in the illustration above. Cut the worm into 10 numbered sections plus the face. Children put the pieces of the puzzle together.

SHADOW ANIMALS

Using the patterns included on page 212, make a gameboard in which the children can match a picture of a farm animal to it's shadow.

EGG CARTON COUNTING

With a marker, label the bottom of each section of an egg carton with a number from 1 to 12. Have small cut-out circles of paper available which are labeled with the same numbers for the children to match.

Another game would be placing the correct number of beans, buttons or seeds in each section.

SHADOW ANIMAL PATTERNS

Directions are found on page 211.

SOUND

Airplanes

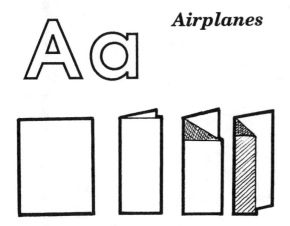

Make paper airplanes to fly out-doors. Begin with a rectangular piece of paper. Fold it in half lengthwise. Then fold one corner back so the top of the page is on the fold. Fold again so that this fold is on the lengthwise fold. Do the same with the other half of the paper. Bring the airplanes outdoors to fly.

Applesauce Cookies

3/4 cup shortening
1 cup brown sugar
1 egg
1/2 cup applesauce
2 1/4 cups flour
1/2 tsp. soda
1/2 tsp. salt
3/4 tsp. cinnamon
1/4 tsp. cloves
1 cup raisins
1/2 cup chopped nuts

Mix together shortening, brown sugar and egg. Stir in applesauce. Sift together flour, salt, and spices; stir in. Mix raisins and nuts. Drop by teaspoonsful onto greased cookie sheet. Bake at 375°for 10 - 12 minutes. Yield: 4 - 5 dozen.

Red

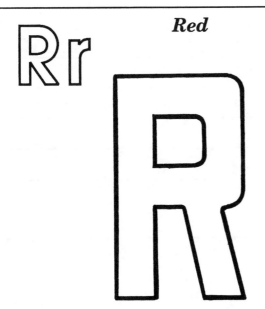

Cut a large "R" out of heavy paper. Have the children cut pictures of red things out of magazines and glue onto the "R" or have them color the "R" red.

Rainbows

Cut out five different-sized half circles from various colors of construction paper. Children glue them together with the largest circle on the bottom and each circle getting progressively smaller.

LIBRARY

Make Way For Ducklings	by Robert McClosky
Night In The Country	by Cynthia Rylant
The Little Tiny Rooster	by Will & Nicolas
Wake Up, Farm	by Alvin Tresselt
I Know A Farm	by Ethel Collier
Pigs Say Oink	by Martha Alexander

MUSIC

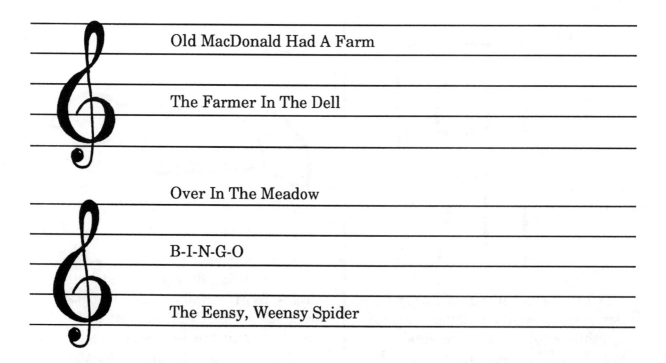

Old MacDonald Had A Farm

The Farmer In The Dell

Over In The Meadow

B-I-N-G-O

The Eensy, Weensy Spider

ART

BARNS AND SILOS

Using the patterns included on pages 216 and 217, make barns to hang on your barnyard window scene.

Explain to the children that real silos are used to store food for the farmer's animals.

VEGETABLE AND FRUIT PAINTING

Bring in a number of raw fruits and vegetables. Cut them into various shapes. Mix up paints in shallow containers. Children dip the fruits and vegetables into the paints and press onto paper. Encourage the children to try and make a face with the food shapes such as the one in the illustration.

BARN PATTERN

Directions are found on page 215.

SILO PATTERN

Directions are found on page 215.

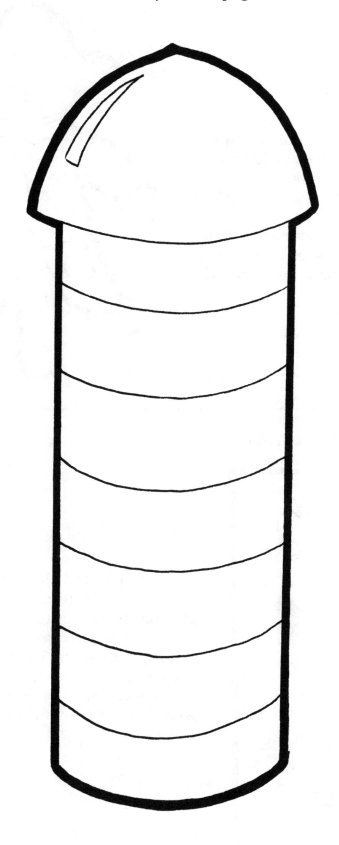

ART

SCARECROW

Enlarge and reproduce this scarecrow pattern for each child. Then children color the scarecrows, cut them out and attach to a popsicle stick to make a scarecrow puppet.

For an extra fun classroom activity have the children "help" make a real scarecrow. Ask parents to donate old clothing and straw.

FOODS GROWN ON A FARM

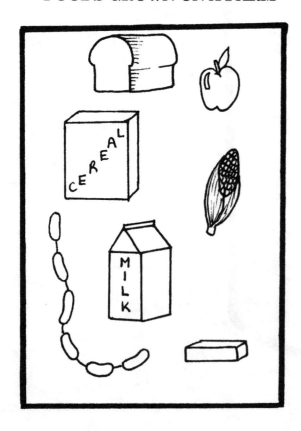

Give each child a large piece of paper and a stack of magazines. Have the children cut out pictures of foods that are grown on farms as well as products created from those foods. This project should be done towards the end of the month when children are more familiar with all of the things which are produced on a farm.

CLASS ACTIVITIES

A PETTING ZOO

Take a field trip to a zoo which has a petting zoo section. Farm animals are usually present there for children to pet and sometimes feed. If you live in a rural area, try to arrange for a field trip to a real farm. May is planting season in many areas so children may be able to see the beginning stages of fields and gardens.

COFFEE CAN ICE CREAM

1 cup whipping cream
1 cup milk
1 egg
1/2 cup sugar
Flavoring - mix all with mixer

Pour mixture into 1 lb. coffee can. Put on the lid. Put the filled 1 lb. coffee can into a 3 lb. coffee can. Add ice cubes and rock salt. Put on the lid. Wrap in a dish towel and shake for 15 to 20 minutes.

WATERMELON

Purchase a watermelon for a special snack on a hot day! Eat outdoors to avoid sticky tables and floors. If you wish to save the seeds, wash them and use them for the watermelon math game on page 211.

If you are feeling especially ambitious, make watermelon pickles with the rinds.

FIELD TRIP

Take a field trip to a local dairy. If a **dairy** is not available in your area take a field trip to a neighborhood bakery. Most bakeries and dairies are willing to give tours and samples if you call ahead and arrange a date and time to bring your class.

A STRAWBERRY PATCH

Plan a field trip to a strawberry patch and allow the children to pick their own strawberries. When you get back to the center, use some of the strawberries to make strawberry jam or strawberry pie.

WHOLE WHEAT MUFFINS

1/4 cup white flour	1 egg
1/4 cup sugar	1 cup milk
4 tsp. baking powder	3 tbls. oil
1 cup whole wheat flour	1 tsp. salt

Mix white flour, salt, sugar, baking powder, and whole wheat flour together. Add egg, milk, and oil. Blend well. Pour batter into paper-lined muffin tins. Bake at 425° for 15 - 18 minutes. Yield: 1 dozen.

SUMMER CAMP

June

Sunday	Monday	Tuesday	Wednesday	Thursday	Friday	Saturday
			1	2	3	4
5	6	7	8	9	10	11
12	13	14	15	16		

For your June calendar, make a large "SUMMER CAMP" banner and a road leading to the camp. Reproduce this log cabin pattern on brown construction paper and label with numbers.

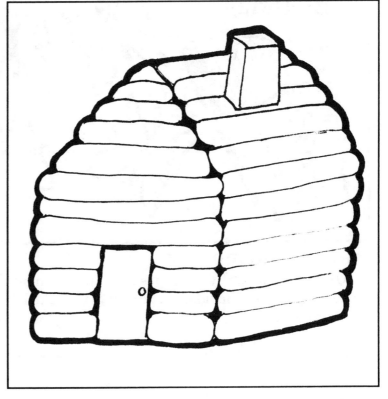

JUNE
BULLETIN BOARDS

PARENT BOARD

Make a river scene on this month's Parent Board by cutting a river, trees and row boats out of construction paper. Label the trees with the Parent Board letters for the heading.

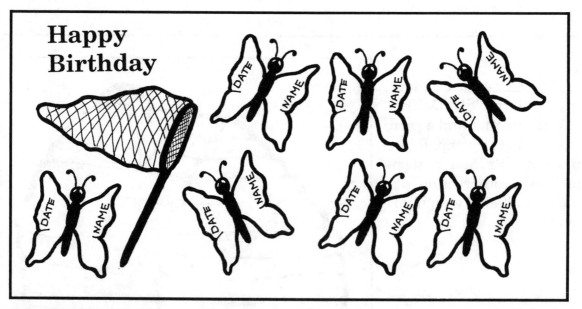

BIRTHDAY BOARD

Use a real butterfly net if possible on this month's Birthday Board. Use the butterfly patterns included on page 232 to make labels for the children's names and birthdates.

WINDOW SCENE

Paint brown trees on your window or use construction paper to make the trees. Cut large green leaves out of construction paper to tape onto the trees to give the appearance of being in the woods. *(The leaf pattern is included on page 226.)*

LEAF PATTERN
FOR THE WINDOW SCENE
Directions are found on page 225.

CUBBY LABEL
Bumble Bee

TABLE LABEL
Back Pack

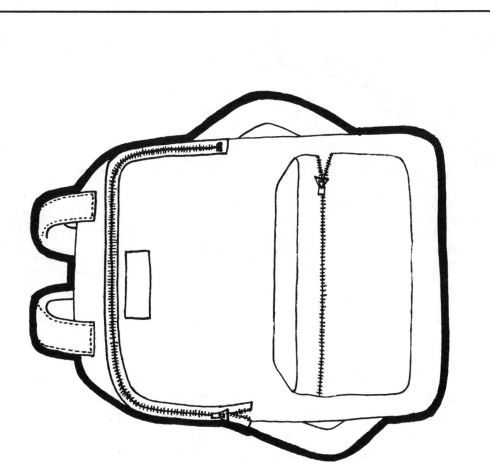

Plans and Patterns for Preschool

T.S. Denison & Co., Inc.

DRAMATIC PLAY

Set up a camping corner for your Dramatic Play area this month. Begin by painting trees on the wall or making them with construction paper. If possible, put a large piece of artificial grass on the floor. Set up a small tent for the children. Inside, have sleeping bags, lanterns, canteens, a first aid kit, and cooking utensils. Parents will probably be willing to loan you most of these materials.

SCIENCE

INSECT BOOKS

Check out books on insects from your local library. Read them to your students and discuss. Have the books available for the children to examine at the science table.

FIRE SAFETY

Discuss fire safety. If possible, visit a nearby fire station or have a fire fighter come and visit your class.

Involve parents by promoting fire safety at home.

WHAT TO EAT WHILE CAMPING?

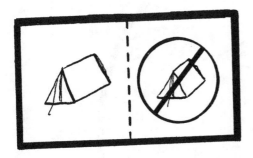

Discuss foods which are good to take camping and why. Cut a number of food pictures from magazines. Have the children decide whether or not each food is good for camping and place it on the appropriate labeled side of the game board. *(The game board is included on page 230.)*

ROCK SAMPLES

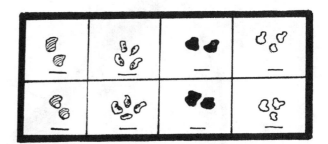

Bring in a variety of rock samples for the children to examine. If you wish, make a chart such as the one above. Put various types of rocks in each square of the top row, then the children find rocks of the same type to put in the bottom row.

THE "WHAT TO EAT WHILE CAMPING" GAME BOARD

Direction are found on page 229.

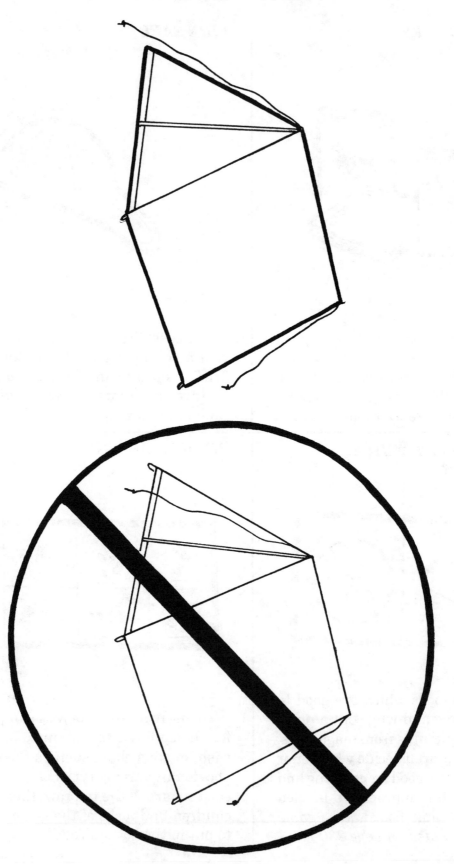

MATH

ROCK COUNTING

Have a collection of small rocks or pebbles at your math center along with paper cups labeled with numbers from 1 to 10. Children place the correct number of rocks into each cup.

BUTTERFLY MATH

Use the patterns included on page 232 to make 10 or more butterflies for this math game. Children match the number of shapes on the left to the number printed on the right to put the butterflies together.

LOG CABINS

Use the log cabin patterns on page 233 to make the log cabins for this math activity. The children arrange the log cabins according to size and number; 1 being the smallest and 10 being the largest.

CANTEEN COUNTING

Using 10 numbered cut-outs of canteens *(pattern found on page 234)*, have the children give each one the appropriate number of drops of water.

BUTTERFLY MATH

Directions are found on page 231.

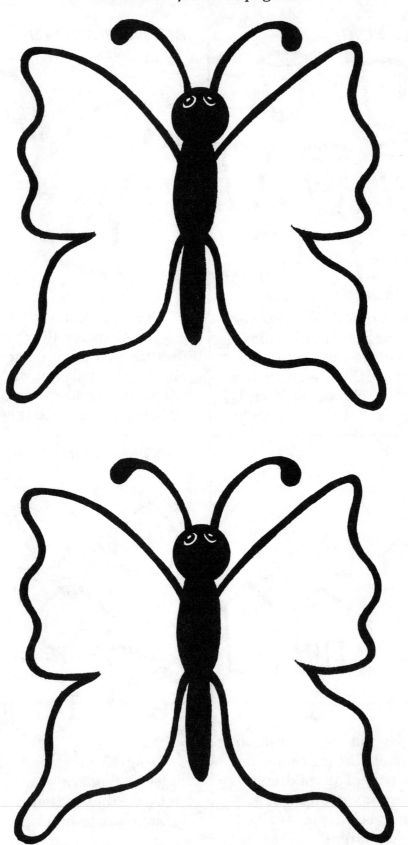

LOG CABINS

Directions are found on page 231.

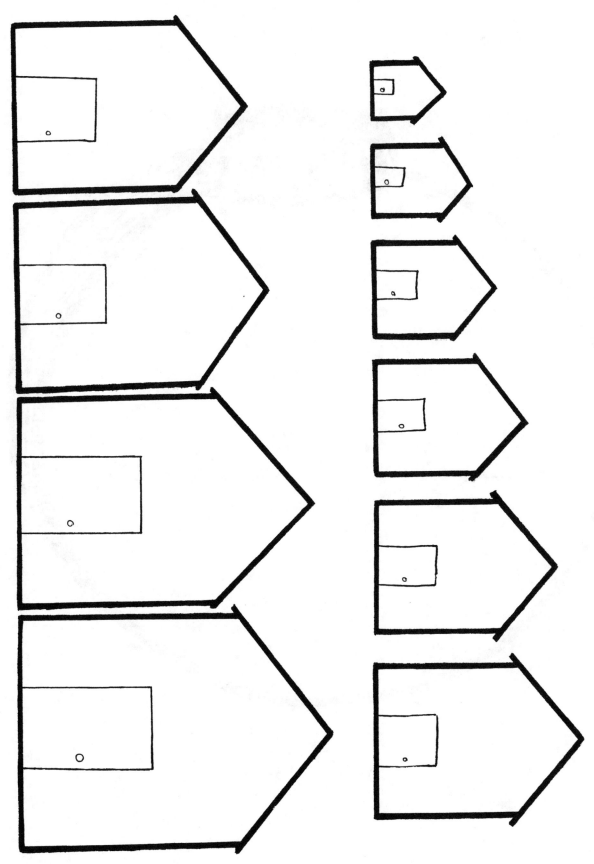

CANTEEN COUNTING

Directions are found on page 231.

SOUND

Eraser Pictures

Begin your eraser pictures by drawing, with a pencil, a simple picture on a large piece of brightly colored construction paper. Have the children erase over the pencil lines until the paper turns white and the picture is easily visible.

Eggs

Fry eggs outdoors as one might do while camping. Begin by building a small fire with sticks in a place where the fire will not spread. Attach clothespins to the top rim of a coffee can. Turn the can upside down so that it is standing on the clothes pins. Spread a little butter on the can and fry your eggs.

SPECIAL NOTE: Recruit extra adults for this activity. Your attention will be on the fire. Recruit others to have their attention on the children.

Tents

Cut a large "T" out of heavy paper for each child. Have the children cut out pictures of tents from camping magazines or catalogs to glue on their "T's."

The children may also enjoy printing small "T's" inside a large "T." A pattern is included on page 237.

Trees

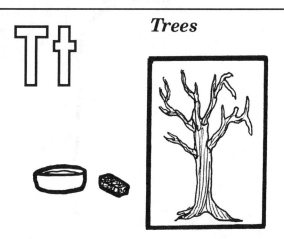

Give each child an outline of a tree with no leaves. The pattern for this tree is provided on page 236. Provide the children with sponges cut into the shape of small leaves. The children dip the sponges into a shallow dish of green paint and then press onto the tree branches to cover the branches with leaves.

TREES

Directions are found on page 235.

PRINT A "T"

Directions are found on page 235.

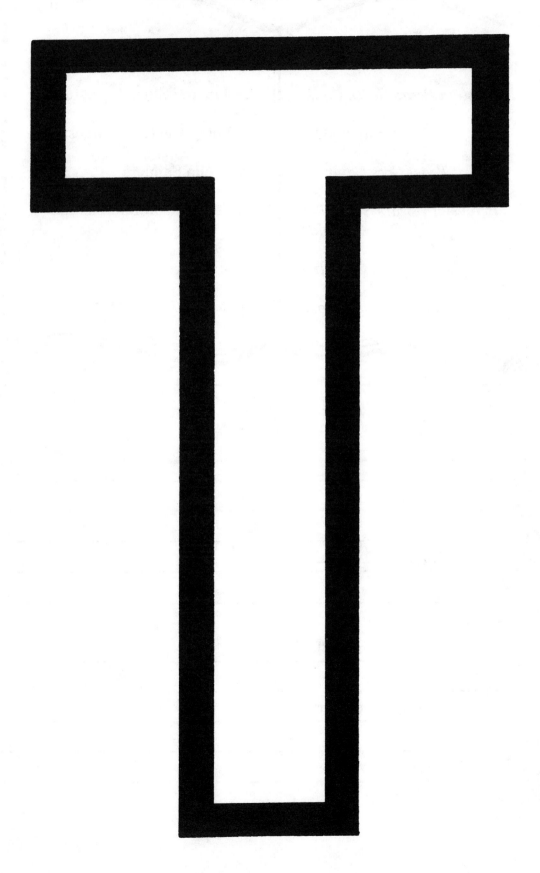

LIBRARY

Camping Adventure	by William R. Gray
The Berenstain Bears Go To Camp	by Jan and Stan Berenstain
Camping Out	by Betsy and Guilio Maestro
Beast Goes Camping	by Sheila Sanders
The Berenstain Bears Shoot The Rapids	by Stan and Jan Berenstain
Gordon Goes Camping	by Julie Brinckloe
A Day In The Woods	by Ronald M. Fisher

MUSIC

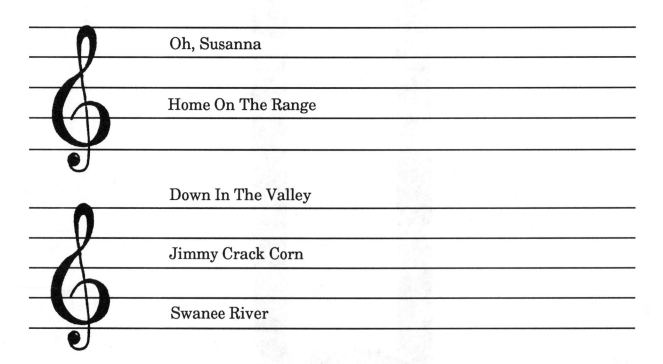

Oh, Susanna

Home On The Range

Down In The Valley

Jimmy Crack Corn

Swanee River

ART

CANDLE MAKING

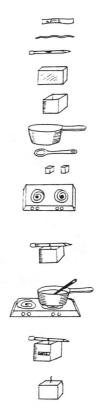

Candle making is a fun project that requires very close supervision. Begin by giving each child a piece of tape with his/her name on it, a piece of string, a pencil, a bar of wax, and the square bottom section of a small milk carton.

Put the tape on the milk carton. Tie the string around the pencil and set the pencil on the milk carton, so the string hangs into the carton, barely touching the bottom.

Using a heavy kettle or double-boiler *(a double-boiler works best)*, heat the wax on a portable burner, stirring constantly until the wax is melted. Add colors and scents *(available at most craft stores).*

Remove from heat and carefully pour into the milk cartons. Allow them to cool for 24 hours. Snip the string (or wick) just below the pencil and peel the carton away from the wax. Candles are then ready to burn or use for decoration!

(This project works best when done with a small group of children.)

SOAP CARVING

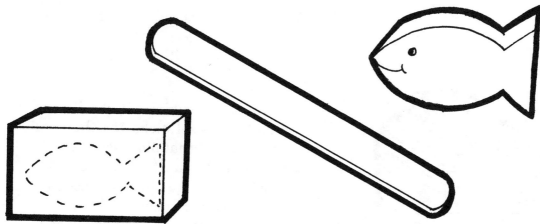

Allow your students to try their hand at carving by experimenting with a bar of soap and a wooden popsicle stick. You will need to draw the shape on the soap for each student by scraping a line with a knife or scissors. The children then carve the soap around the shape with the popsicle stick.

A soft soap bar such as Ivory works best. Start out with very simple pictures or shapes with as few lines as possible.

ART

ROCK PAPERWEIGHTS

Make paper wieghts out of rocks! Begin by having each child bring in a rock. Scrub the rock clean with soap and water. Decorate the rocks by painting a picture on them. This art project could be used as a Father's Day gift.

PRETZEL LOG CABINS

Make log cabins out of milk cartons and pretzel sticks. Use the small milk cartons that most schools have available at lunch. Children glue pretzel sticks to them to resemble logs. Construction paper doors, windows and a chimney can be added to the log cabins.

CLASS ACTIVITIES

S'MORES

Make indoor s'mores by placing a chocolate candy bar or chocolate chips and marshmallows between two graham crackers. Heat over a gas stove burner or in a microwave oven until the chocolate and marshmallows are warm and soft.

NATURE HIKE

Take a nature hike through the woods. Give each child a bag in which to collect natural "treasures."

If you live in an area where there are no woods nearby, do the same sort of activity at a park.

A CENTER CAMP OUT (INDOORS)

Make plans for a center campout. Have parents lend you tents, sleeping bags and food. Be sure that all safety precautions are taken and have plenty of adult supervision. An indoor camp out can be lots of fun. If you prefer not to try this activity, turn rest-time into a camping experience.

GRILL LUNCH

Build a real fire or use a grill and roast hot dogs for lunch one day. Roast marshmallows for dessert!

GORP

Gorp is a snack that most campers are familiar with. Make your own gorp by mixing together some of the children's favorite dry foods, such as cereals, M&M's, peanuts, raisins and pretzels.

DRY APPLES

Dry apples for a tasty and nutritious snack. Cut an apple into eight sections. Remove the seeds and string them from the ceiling for two or three days or until dry. If possible, borrow a dehydrater and dry a variety of fruits for snacks.

JULY

AT THE BEACH

July

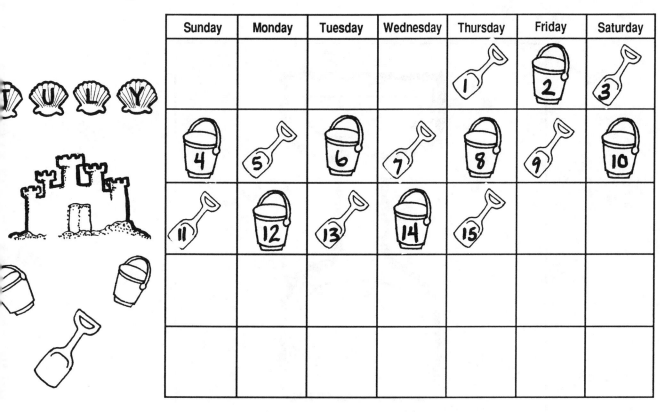

Sunday	Monday	Tuesday	Wednesday	Thursday	Friday	Saturday
				1	2	3
4	5	6	7	8	9	10
11	12	13	14	15		

Enlarge the sandcastle on light brown paper to create the setting for this "AT THE BEACH" calendar. Use the seashell patterns *(on following page)* provided to make the "JULY" heading.

Reproduce this sand pail pattern as well as the shovel pattern *(on following page)* and label them with the numbers between 1 and 31.

CALENDAR PATTERNS

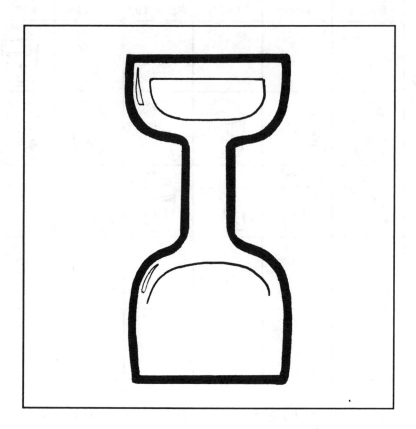

JULY
BULLETIN BOARDS

PARENT BOARD

Begin this Parent Board with a light blue background and a green border. Enlarge and color the mermaid and write the Parent Board heading on her chalk board. You may also want to make bubbles to increase the "underwater" feeling.

BIRTHDAY BOARD

Make a bright yellow sun to hang in the corner of July's Birthday Board. Reproduce a pair of sunglasses for each child on brightly colored construction paper. Label the glasses with the children's names and birthdates. This is a special treat for the children when it comes time to take them home at the end of the month.

SUNGLASSES PATTERN
FOR THE BIRTHDAY BOARD
Directions are found on page 247.

WINDOW SCENE

Paint blue water on the bottom portion of the window and a bright yellow sun at the top. White clouds can either painted on the window or made from white paper with cotton glued on to the paper. Make sailboats as an art project to finish the seaside scenery. *(Sailboat pattern is found on page 258.)*

CUBBY LABEL
Seashell

TABLE LABEL
Beach Ball

Plans and Patterns for Preschool

T.S. Denison & Co., Inc.

DRAMATIC PLAY

Create a beach scene in your classroom. Paint or use construction paper to decorate your walls with waves, sunshine, and clouds. Use some of the sailboats from the art project on page 257 to sail on the waves. Include beach towels, beach balls, a radio, empty bottles of sun screen lotion, and a picnic lunch.

SCIENCE

SINK OR FLOAT

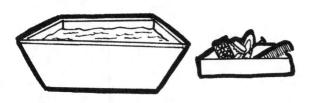

Have a sink or float experiment set up in your science center this month. You will need a basin of water and a box full of small objects such as paper clips, bottle caps, pieces of fabric, corks or whatever else you can find. The children determine whether the object will sink or float and then test their decision by placing the object in the pan of water.

AQUARIUM

If you don't already have an aquarium in the classroom this would be a good month to acquire one. You can purchase an inexpensive aquarium and a few small fish from a local pet store. Give the children the responsibility of feeding the fish and keeping the aquarium clean. Have books available about fish for the children to examine.

WATER SAFETY

Discuss the importance of water safety:

1. Always wear a life jacket or flotation device.
2. Always use the buddy system while at a pool or lake.
3. Always sit down while in a boat and wear a life preserver.
4. Take swimming lessons to learn how to swim.
5. Never dive into shallow water.
6. Stay away from pools and lakes during stormy weather.

SHELLS

Place a number of sea shells on your science table. Ask children to bring shells from home if you do not have any.

MATH

MEASURING SAND

Put a pan of clean sand on your math table during the month of July. Have a number of measuring spoons and cups available for the children to experiment with.

LIGHTHOUSE PUZZLE

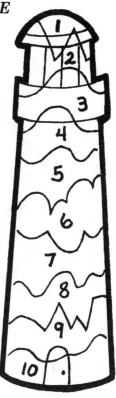

Enlarge this lighthouse pattern on white poster board. Cut into 10 puzzle pieces as shown. Children put them together in numerical order and find that they have put together a lighthouse.

HOW MANY FISH CAN THE PELICAN EAT?

Make a very large pelican such as the one pictured here. Attach a paper bag behind the beak. Have cards with different numbers available to tape to the front of his beak to tell the children how many fish to feed the pelican. The fish pattern is included on page 254.

ROW BOATS

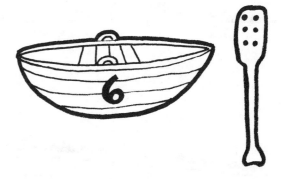

Make 10 row boats and 10 oars. Number the boats from 1 to 10. On the oars put dots which correspond to the number on the boat. Children match the number on each boat to the correct oar.

PATTERNS FOR THE
MATH ACTIVITIES

Featured on page 253.

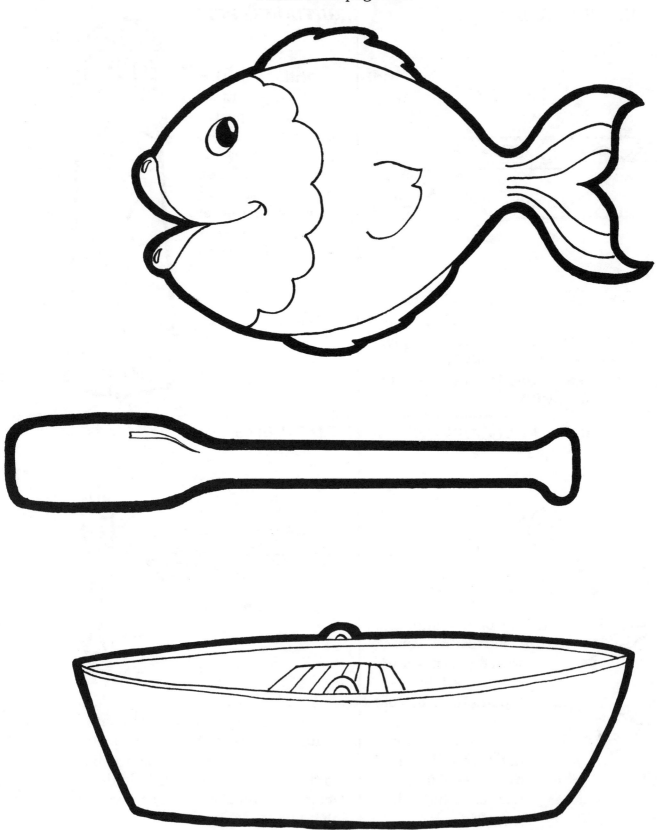

SOUND

Fishing

Make a fishing game to keep in your sound center during July. You can easily make a fishing pole by tying a magnet on one end of a string and tying the other end of a string to a dowel rod or stick.

Attach paper clips to fish cutouts, some labeled with the letter "F" and some labeled with other letters. Have the children throw back any fish that are not labeled with an "F."

Fans

Teach your students how to make fans by folding colorful paper back and forth. Secure with a piece of tape at the bottom.

Orange

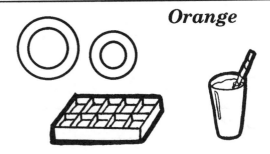

Make a very healthy snack by freezing orange juice in an ice cube tray. Put a stick into each section before the juice is completely frozen. How much fun to enjoy orange juice popsicles on a hot July day.

Another fun snack is to make an orange shake. In a blender mix: 6 oz. can of frozen orange juice; 1 cup milk; 1 cup water; 1/2 cup sugar; 1 tsp. vanilla; 10 or 12 ice cubes. Makes 6 cups.

Octopus

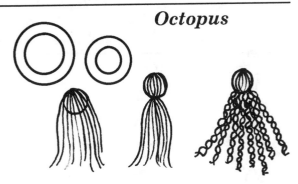

(For best results do this project with one or two children at a time.)

Allow each student to make his or her own octopus by wrapping yarn around a styrofoam ball and tying it together close to the ball, forming the head of the octopus. Divide the hanging yarn into eight sections. Braid each section and tie at knot at the bottom. Glue on movable eyes and a red yarn mouth.

LIBRARY

Swimmy	by Leo Lionni
Harry By The Sea	by Gene Zion
In Summer	by Jane Belk Moncure and Aileen Fisher
A Day Of Summer	by Betty Miles
Fish Is Fish	by Leo Lionni
Paddington At The Seaside	by Michael Bond and Fred Banbery

MUSIC

Row, Row, Row Your Boat

My Bonnie Lies Over The Ocean

Sailing, Sailing

ART

SAILBOATS

Use the patterns included on page 258 to make sailboats. The children glue wooden popsicle sticks to the back of each sail and then glue them to the back of the boat.

Hang some of the sailboats on your window scene and some of them in your dramatic play area.

WHALES

Enlarge this pattern of a whale and make a copy of it for every child in your class. Allow the children to color, paint or decorate their whales as they please. Punch a hole in the top of the whale and tie a string. Hang the whales from the ceiling.

SAILBOAT PATTERN

Directions are found on page 257.

ART

PUFF-PAINT SHIRTS

Ask your students to bring in a t-shirt from home that does not have any pictures or printing on it; a plain t-shirt. Purchase puff-paints at a craft store and allow the students to create their own designs for their shirts. Let the paint dry overnight.

Let the children have a style show with the "fancy" new shirts.

COLORED SAND JARS

Purchase a number of colors of sand at a craft store. Parents with babies will probably be able to provide you with small baby food jars.

Each child will pour alternating colors of sand into their jars to create interesting designs.

CLASS ACTIVITIES

BEACH PARTY

Have a beach party! Hang a big banner outside with balloons and streamers to create a party atmosphere. Children bring swimsuits and towels from home. Have children's wading pools, water slides, and sprinklers set up for the children to enjoy. You could also have music playing and sunglasses available. *(Be sure to recruit extra help from the parents!)*

SAILING BOATS

Make sailboats that really work! Give each child a small flat piece of styrofoam, a toothpick and a triangular piece of paper. Show the children how to stick the toothpick through the paper in order to create a sail. Then stick the toothpick into the styrofoam to complete the boat. Sail them in a sink or a large container of water.

SUMMER SWIMMING LESSONS

If you have a pool in your neighborhood, try to arrange to take your class for swimming lessons during the summer. Most parents really appreciate this effort.

BUBBLES

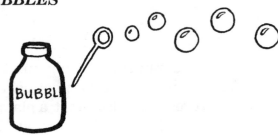

Buy a few bottles of inexpensive bubbles and let the children blow bubbles outdoors. Create games involving catching or counting the bubbles.

HANDPRINTS

Make handprints and/or footprints with paint, large pieces of paper, and a lot of water. In order to avoid a very messy classroom, do this activity outdoors. Be sure all the paint is washed off before going back into the school.

MUSEUM

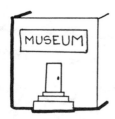

Visit an Aquatic Museum and examine the various types of exotic fish. If this is not possible, take your class fishing at a nearby lake. **(Bring a lot of adult help with you!)**

AUGUST

August

CALENDAR

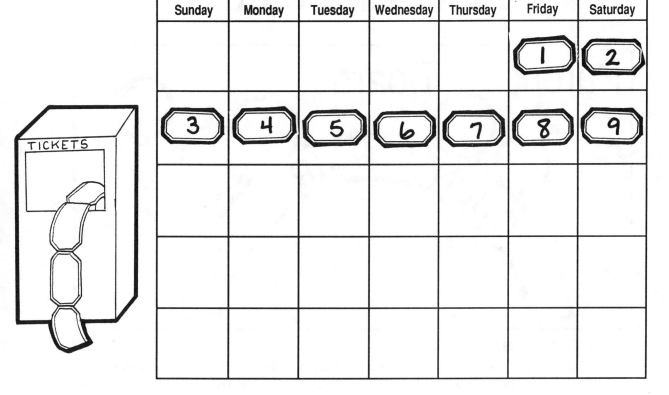

Sunday	Monday	Tuesday	Wednesday	Thursday	Friday	Saturday
					1	2
3	4	5	6	7	8	9

Make a large ticket booth out of large paper or poster board. Reproduce the ticket pattern on a variety of colored paper. Number them from 1 to 31.

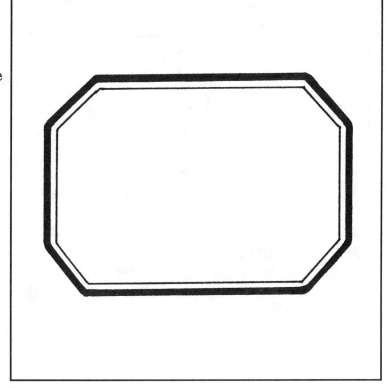

AUGUST
BULLETIN BOARDS

PARENT BOARD

 Make a large COUNTY FAIR banner for August's Parent Board. Hang real or construction paper balloons around the banner to help create the County Fair atmosphere.

BIRTHDAY BOARD

 Make a large ferris wheel for this month's Birthday Board. Cut colorful cars out of construction paper and label them with the children's names and birthdates.

WINDOW SCENE

Begin this window scene with a brightly colored border. Enlarge the clown pattern above on poster board and color. Finally, put strings on paper or real balloons and attach them with tape to the window for the clown to hold.

CUBBY LABEL
Ice Cream Cone

Plans and Patterns for Preschool

TABLE LABEL
First Place Ribbon

1ST PLACE

T.S. Denison & Co., Inc.

DRAMATIC PLAY

Make a duck pond game in your dramatic play area this month. You will need a pan of water and small plastic ducks. Mark the bottom of each duck with a number. Children choose a duck and then win a prize according to the number found on it.

SCIENCE

SODA BOTTLE BALLOON

A balloon can be blown up on a soda bottle. Stretch the balloon opening on top of the bottle opening. Then place the bottle in a pan of water and heat slowly over a portable burner. As the water heats the bottle, the air inside it will expand causing the balloon to be blown up. Be sure you remove the balloon or remove the pan from the heat before the balloon pops!

Remember: Always use a great deal of caution when performing science experiments with young children.

SUN BLEACHED PAPER

Write each child's name on a piece of colored construction paper. Set the paper outside on a sunny day with a number of objects on each paper. The children will be excited to find the picture that results when the sun bleaches the areas around the objects but not the areas under the objects.

MAGNETS

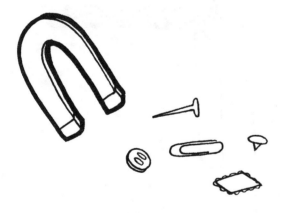

Place a magnet and a number of small objects on your science table during the month of August. Allow the children to experiment and discover which objects can and cannot be picked up with a magnet.

MAGNIFYING GLASS OR MICROSCOPE

Place a magnifying glass or microscope on your science table. Provide the children with a variety of samples for your children to examine; newspaper, foods, yarn, rocks, leaves and flowers

MATH

GUESS

Have a number of jars filled with candy, gum, or small toys sitting on your math table this month. The children guess how many of each object are in each jar. Write the children's guesses down on a piece of paper. *(They may need help with this.)* The child who guesses the closest to the correct number wins the jar and shares the contents with the rest of the class.

RING TOSS

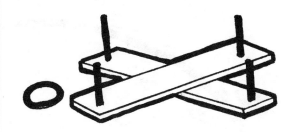

Use a purchased ring toss game or make your own by sticking wooden dowel rods in an X-shaped piece of styrofoam, using a ring made by cutting out the inside of a coffee can lid. Children set a timer for 2 or 3 minutes and count how many times their ring lands around a rod before the bell rings.

BALLOONS

Use the pattern included on page 270 to make this math game. Children count the number of designs on the decorated balloons, then set them on top of the correctly numbered balloons.

DOT-TO-DOT ICE CREAM

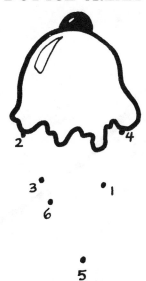

Use the pattern included on page 271 to make this dot-to-dot game for each child. Children connect the dots between the numbers 1 to 10. Color the ice cream cones.

BALLOON PATTERN

Directions are found on page 269.

ICE CREAM DOT-TO-DOT

Directions are found on page 269.

SOUND

Bb *Blue Balloons*

For a special treat, give each of your students a helium-filled balloon. Write "Bb" on each of the balloons with a permanent marker to reinforce the sound.

Bb *Beans*

Buy a box or two of dried beans at your grocery store. Allow the children to glue the beans onto a drawing of the letter "B." "B" pattern is included on page 273.

Nn *Newspaper N's*

Provide stencils of an upper case "N" and a lower case "n" made out of poster board. Children trace the letters onto newspaper and cut them out. Glue the newspaper "n's" on a piece of black construction paper.

Nn *Noodle Necklaces*

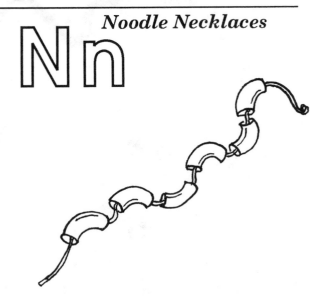

Provide different kinds of macaroni noodles for the children to string onto a piece of yarn. Help the children tie the ends together to make necklaces.

LETTER "B"

Directions are found on page 272.

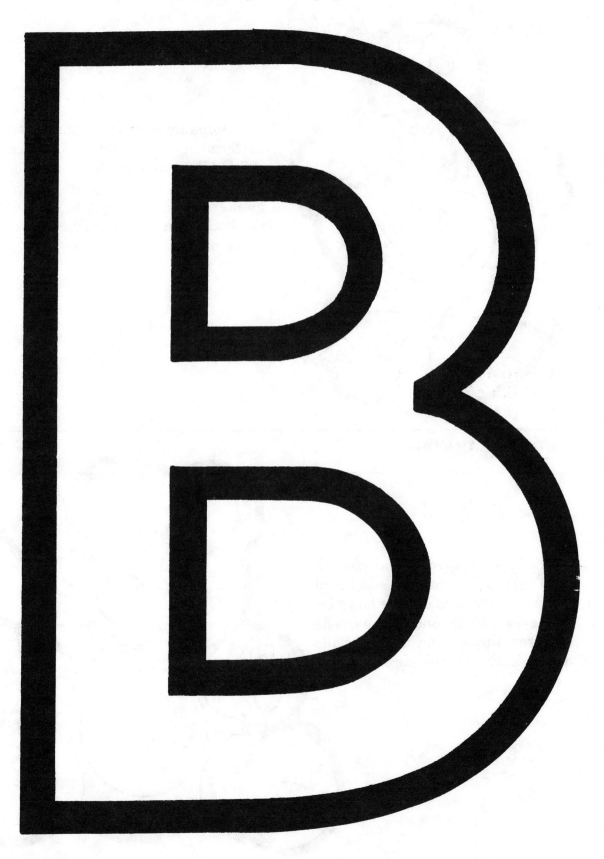

ART

CLOWNS

Reproduce a copy of this clown pattern on heavy paper for each child. Allow your students to color their clowns with brightly colored markers. Attach a popsicle stick to the back with glue to make a cute clown puppet.

TEDDY BEAR TOSS

Enlarge this teddy bear pattern on a very large piece of poster board or card board. Cut out the holes for the eyes, mouth and tummy. The children throw bean bags or balls through the holes to score points.

ART

MERRY-GO-ROUND

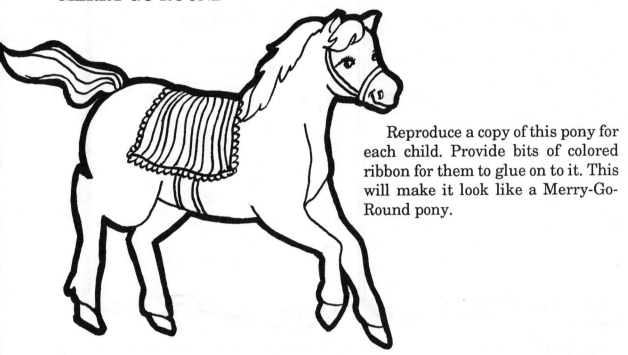

Reproduce a copy of this pony for each child. Provide bits of colored ribbon for them to glue on to it. This will make it look like a Merry-Go-Round pony.

DECORATE BALLOONS

Give each child a large balloon and have them decorate it with stickers or shapes cut out of colored construction paper.

LIBRARY

Stumpy Goes To The Fair   by Ursula Hourihane

The Marvelous Merry-Go-Round   by Dahlov Ipcar

Chester   by Syd Hoff

MUSIC

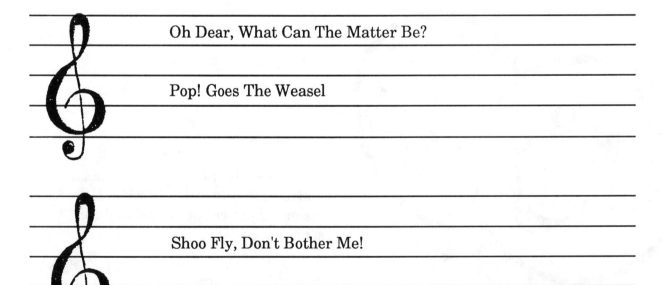

Oh Dear, What Can The Matter Be?

Pop! Goes The Weasel

Shoo Fly, Don't Bother Me!

CLASS ACTIVITIES

TALENT SHOW

Involve your whole center in putting together a talent show for the parents. Have each class do a skit or sing songs. Make it a fun activity and not a contest.

PET SHOW

Allow your students to bring their pets to school for a pet show. Make sure that each pet receives some sort of prize, such as:
- the largest pet
- smallest pet
- quietest pet
- cutest pet
- most unusual pet
- best-trained pet
- furriest pet

CLOWN PICTURES

Make a large picture of a clown on very heavy poster board. *(See illustration.)* Paint the clown face with bright colors. Make the hole in the face large enough for a child's face to fit through. Have each child stand behind the clown with their face making up the face of the clown. Use make-up if desired. Take polaroid pictures.

CARAMELED POPCORN

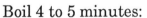

Boil 4 to 5 minutes:
- 2 cups brown sugar
- 1/2 cup butter
- 1/2 cup corn syrup
- 1 tsp salt

• Add 1/2 tsp baking soda, 1 tsp vanilla. Pour over 6 cups of popped corn and bake one hour at 250°. Nuts may be added.

THE COUNTY FAIR

If possible, take a field trip to a County fair, State Fair, or Amusement Park. Or consider having a fair at your center, including games, shows and snacks.

BEAN BAG GAME

Make a bean bag toss game such as this one out of card board. Add up each child's points according to which hole his/her bean bag lands in.

Monthly Reproducible Parent Notices

*(May be used on the Parent Board each month,
or may be used as individual notes that are sent home with the children.)*

September
News

OCTOBER
NEWS

_____

_____

_____

_____

_____

_____

_____

_____

_____

_____

_____

_____

_____

November
News

_____
_____
_____
_____

_____

_____

_____

_____

_____

_____

_____

_____

_____

_____

_____

_____

_____

_____

_____

_____

December
News

January
News

February
News

_____

_____

_____

_____

_____

_____

_____

_____

_____

_____

_____

_____

_____

_____

_____

_____

March
News

April
News

BREADS AND CEREAL

FRUITS AND VEGETABLES

MEAT

MILK

DAIRY

MAY NEWS

_____

_____

_____

_____

_____

_____

_____

_____

_____

_____

_____

_____

_____

_____

_____

June News

JULY NEWS

_____

_____

_____

_____

_____

_____

_____

_____

_____

_____

_____

_____

_____

_____

_____

AUGUST NEWS

Monthly
Awards

WELCOME TO SCHOOL

Name

Teacher

I Know My Halloween Safety Rules

Name

Teacher

We Are Thankful For You!

From _____

To _____

Date _____

**Thank You
For Being So
Thoughtful!
You Know How To Share**

THE POLAR BEAR AWARD

To _____

For _____

_____

Teacher _____ Date

You Warm My Heart

Name _____

Teacher _____

A "*Springing*" *Good Job!*

Name   Teacher   Date

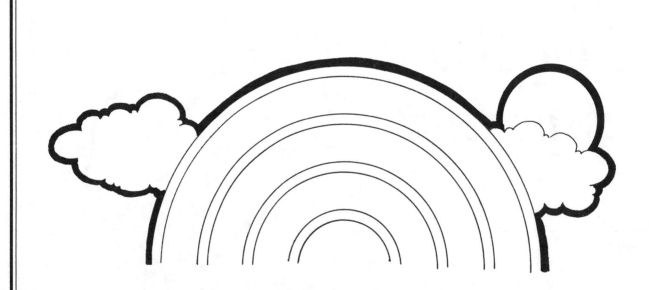

YOU MADE MY DAY FULL OF RAINBOWS

You Brighten My Day!

Name _____

Teacher _____

Date _____

I Had A
WONDERFUL
DAY

Name _____ **Teacher** _____ **Date** _____

A SENSATIONAL SUMMER DAY!

_____
NAME

_____
TEACHER

_____
DATE

Your Teacher Is Very Proud Of You

_____

_____

_____

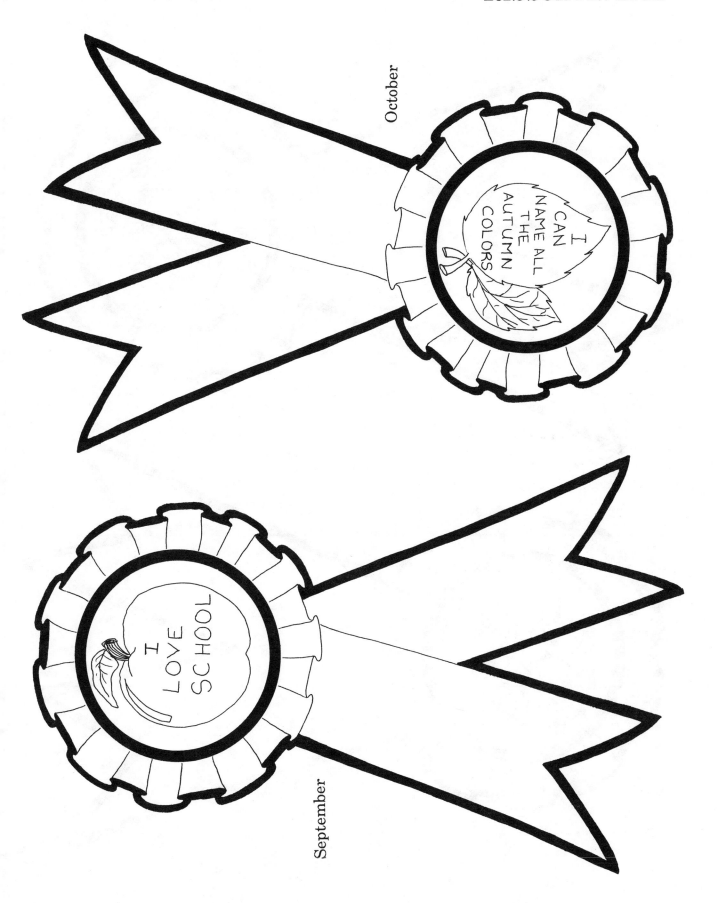

October

I CAN NAME ALL THE AUTUMN COLORS

I LOVE SCHOOL

September

December

November

SANTA'S HELPER IN THE CLASSROOM

I AM THANKFUL FOR

Ribbon Awards

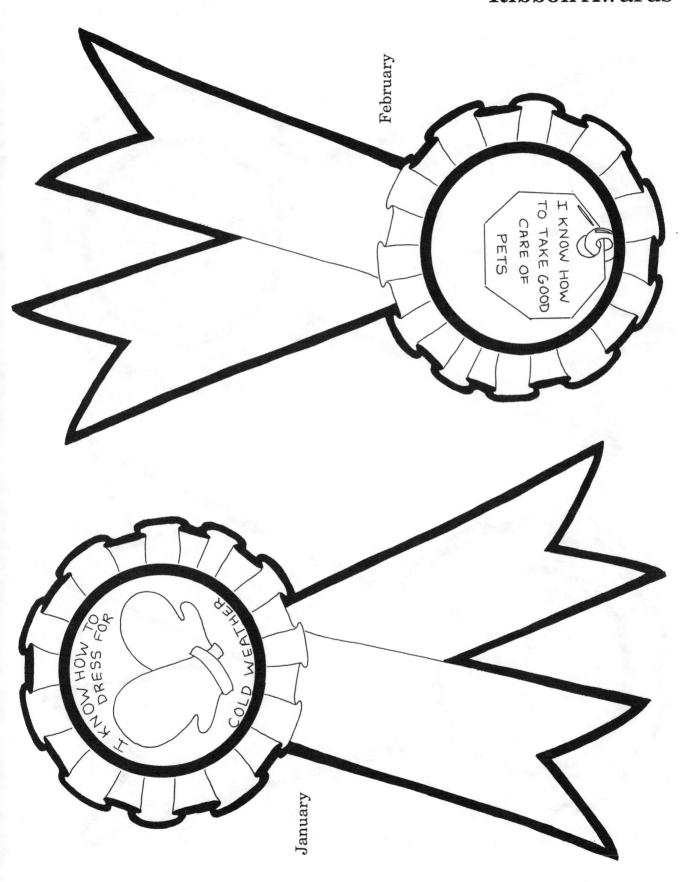

February

I KNOW HOW TO TAKE GOOD CARE OF PETS

I KNOW HOW TO DRESS FOR COLD WEATHER

January

Ribbon Awards

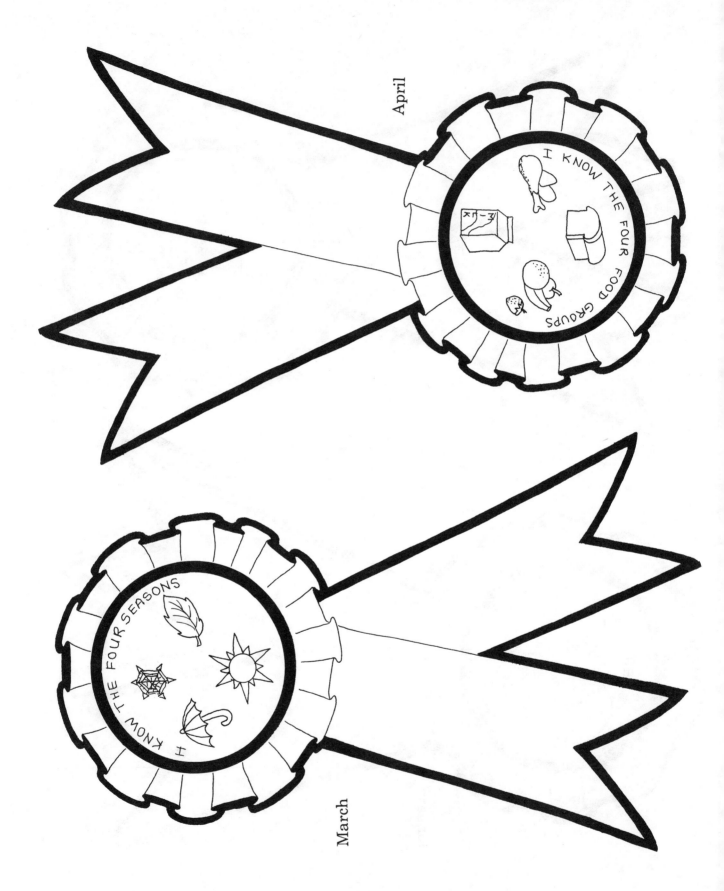

April

I KNOW THE FOUR FOOD GROUPS

March

I KNOW THE FOUR SEASONS

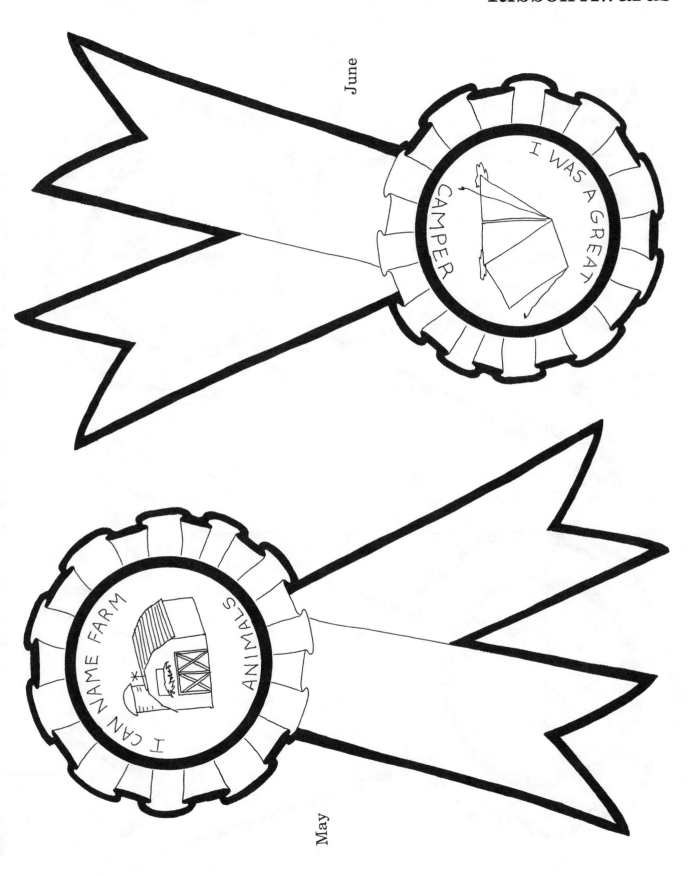

June

CAMPER

I WAS A GREAT

I CAN NAME FARM

ANIMALS

May

Ribbon Awards

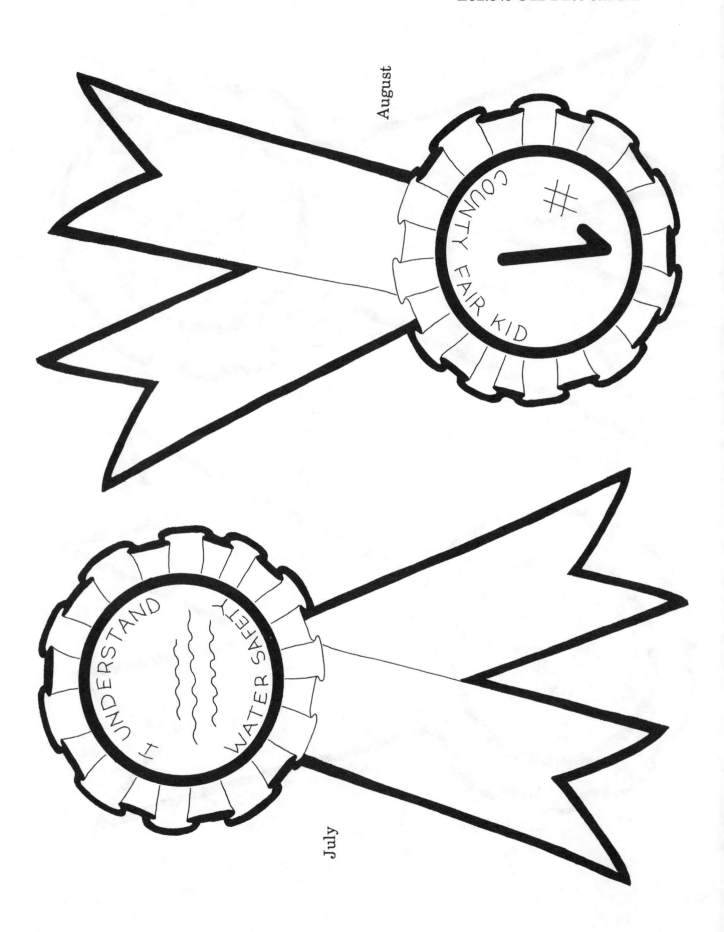

August

COUNTY FAIR KID

#

I UNDERSTAND

WATER SAFETY

July

MONTHLY ACTIVITY CONTENTS

Teacher's Notes . . .

Teacher's Notes . . .

Teacher's Notes . . .

Teacher's Notes . . .

Teacher's Notes . . .

Teacher's Notes . . .

T.S. Denison & Co., Inc. 318 *Plans and Patterns for Preschool*

Teacher's Notes . . .

Teacher's Notes . . .